# THIS BOOK IS RATED "G" as in gee I wish I did this stuff sooner

One always feels sexier when you are successful in business and financially; it breeds confidence and a higher self-esteem - No matter what stage in life you are at, no matter how much or how little money you have, whether you're a family, individual, small or mid-size business. Success doesn't just happen-it takes good organizational skills, hard work, planning, review and changes when needed, **and a good book to help you get there.**

## That Is Why *This Book Is A MUST*

4 things you need IN WRITING: *Your roadmap for <u>personal</u> & <u>business</u> success*

1. A Life Plan (Estate)
2. A Budget/Retirement Budget
3. An investment Plan
4. Business & Personal Succession Plan

How lucky are you, my book covers all 4 and more...

# THE

## Sexy
## Little Book of
# FINANCE
# III

FRANK J. EBERHART, CEP®, RFC®

ARCHWAY
PUBLISHING

Archway Publishing books may be ordered through booksellers or by contacting:

Archway Publishing
1663 Liberty Drive
Bloomington, IN 47403
www.archwaypublishing.com
1-(888)-242-5904

ISBN: 978-1-4808-0842-3 (sc)
ISBN: 978-1-4808-0843-0 (e)

Library of Congress Control Number: 2014910878

Printed in the United States of America.

Archway Publishing rev. date: 6/16/2014

# Contents

# Book 1: Estate Planning

## Control Your Destiny

It's not just about dying and setting up your estate-it is about how you live before you die....

You work hard, save and invest wisely, but alas, you never thought about what happens to your family when you're dead if you are not prepared? Not exactly a pleasant thought (or one we think about on a regular basis), but a necessary one for sure. The consequences for not being prepared can be quite devastating. If you don't each have [1]health care and investment proxies, a valid specific will or trust. A valid will or trust is one that is signed, witnessed and notarized. Dyeing without a valid will or trust is referred to as dyeing intestate-without a will when your family goes to probate court, there is no direction (no will to read) so potentially the state takes over for all your affairs-not a pleasant process. You need to name your beneficiaries to all of your life insurance policies, 401K and IRA'S, savings, or any other financial or property you own. You need to change your will to match your beneficiaries as **your will overrides your beneficiary designations, this is very important especially in cases where there has been a divorce.** If you own a business, a succession plan is crucial-what happens to your business and family?

Most of the items in my book never happen until the need arises, generally through some type of crisis, family issues, law suits, hospital bills, divorce, death etc. Putting off these important decisions is (somewhat) understandable in today's busy environment with both spouses working, self-employment, kid's activities – I know, we have soccer, wrestling, baseball, basketball, dance, I'm self-employed and my wife works; like you, we need that 8th day just for us.

You need an **EASY to UNDERSTAND & EASY METHOD** for *investing, estate planning, and budgeting.*

My 4 step combined workbook will guide you through probate, trusts, understanding duties of executors and trustees, living wills, power of attorney's, budgeting, and investing in an easy fill-in-the-blanks approach. It starts with a plan (in writing); I made it real easy (Hint: just fill in the blanks) add a little knowledge (which I provide), common sense (you have to apply), and research (I show you where and how). Life changes happen all the time, you need all the information this book provides to make and update proper decisions on investments, estate planning, budgeting, retirement, **Medicaid**, **Medicare**, individual and business succession issues. This information is important for your accountant, your attorney, your broker, you, and your family.

---

[1] Durable power of attorney (financial): Allows full or partial authority of an individual to make decisions and transact business on your be-half in the case of incapacitation. The appointment can be by will pro-visions, trust instruments, or court appointment. Durable power of attorney (health care): Allows full or partial authority of an individual to make decisions for health care in the event that you are unable to do so (you are incapacitated). The appointment can be by will provisions, trust instruments, or court appointment.

Financial success doesn't just happen; it takes hard work, good organizational skills, planning, execution, review, and revision when necessary. I have provided direct links for Medicare/Medicaid, Gift Tax, Estate Tax, State Gift and Estate Tax, Tax Tables, Nursing Home Search, Social Security Enrollment, and a whole lot more. I prefer financial *SUCCESS* to financial *STREES*. So let's get started.

TAKE YOUR FINANCES, YOUR ESTATE, YOUR BUSINESS AND YOURSELF TO A NEW LEVEL

*It's not just your future, or your money, it is preparing your family for their future without you*

# Estate Planning Checklist: Personal and Business

The first item that you will need to complete is the estate-planning checklist, which you will find on the next page. You should make copies for changes and updates to your plans and budgets. Put this information in a separate book for your records.

You need to have a current will or trust, establish your living wills, make provisions for executor/executrix of your estate and business, assign a guardian for your children (in the event of simultaneous deaths), name all beneficiaries, and assign any successor trustees (like a bank trust department). Wills, which only become effective after death, and can take 6 months or longer to complete, are public information and anybody can see them. Wills and trusts should be reviewed every three to five years.

Furthermore, a will (or no will-dying intestate) does not provide for incapacitation or the ability to make short-or long-term decisions for yourself; it becomes court appointed in which case the court makes financial decisions on your behalf. So you need proper health and investment proxies, and power of attorney's for you and your spouse (each of you has one) and your business to provide direction for and control of your financial decisions.

*You will also need the following:*
- Safekeeping for children's, you, and your spouse's original birth certificates
- [2]Life insurance for estate taxes and living expenses for surviving spouse
- A copy of your trust or will with all proper insurance policy numbers, brokerage accounts, bank accounts, annuities, and any other investments deemed important—and a video of your wishes to leave no doubt of your intentions—with your attorney or executor
- Life insurance on children (to guarantee insurability)
- Long-term health care provisions, durable power of attorney's for health and investment directives, living wills, you each have to have these items as separate proxies
- Updated adequate homeowner's insurance to reflect current market price
- Mortgage insurance —sometimes a regular life insurance term policy may be less expensive
- Umbrella policy(s) for additional liability coverage on your real estate properties
- Stocks, bonds, and mutual funds (if you own certificates, put them in street name with a brokerage firm Street name means that you hold your securities and stock certificates in a brokerage account versus in your safe deposit box.
- Disability insurance, find out how much it costs and covers and for how long
- Long-term care policies for financial help for nursing home or assisted living facilities
- IRA, life insurance, or other qualified plans—make sure beneficiaries match your will or trusts

---

[2] Page 34-How Much Life Insurance Do You Need?

- Out-of-state property (find out probate rules and whether it's in trust)
- Safe-deposit box or in home safe with copies of social security numbers and birth certificates
- Business succession plan, key-man insurance, buy-sell agreements-determine who takes over in the event of your death
- Current budget review as needed at least annually
- Current retirement budget review at least annually
- Review wills and trusts every 3 to 5 years as the laws and your circumstances may have changed
- A filing system that identifies all categories such as auto, insurance, expenses, credit cards, investments, receipts, and any other pertinent information

## Quick-Reference Contact Information

|  | Doctor | Pediatrician | Dentist |
|---|---|---|---|
| Name | | | |
| Address | | | |
| City, state, ZIP | | | |
| Phone | | | |
| Fax | | | |
| Pager | | | |
| E-mail | | | |
| Cell phone | | | |

|  | Executor | Guardian(s) | Lawyer |
|---|---|---|---|
| Name | | | |
| City, state, ZIP | | | |
| Phone | | | |
| Fax | | | |
| Pager | | | |
| E-mail | | | |
| Cell phone | | | |

|  | Accountant | Funeral director | Bank safe deposit/number |
|---|---|---|---|
| Name | | | |
| Address | | | |
| City, state, ZIP | | | |
| Phone | | | |
| Fax | | | |

Pager      _____      _____      _____

E-mail      _____      _____      _____

Cell phone      _____      _____      _____

## Additional Items for Business:

|  | Suppliers | Bank/Credit Line | Loans |
|---|---|---|---|
| Name | _____ | _____ | _____ |
| Address | _____ | _____ | _____ |
| City, state, ZIP | _____ | _____ | _____ |
| Phone | _____ | _____ | _____ |
| Fax | _____ | _____ | _____ |
| Pager | _____ | _____ | _____ |
| E-mail | _____ | _____ | _____ |
| Cell phone | _____ | _____ | _____ |

|  | Credit Card Processor | 401K/SEP | Health Care Provider |
|---|---|---|---|
| Name | _____ | _____ | _____ |
| Address | _____ | _____ | _____ |
| City, state, ZIP | _____ | _____ | _____ |
| Phone | _____ | _____ | _____ |
| Fax | _____ | _____ | _____ |
| Pager | _____ | _____ | _____ |
| E-mail | _____ | _____ | _____ |
| Cell phone | _____ | _____ | _____ |

Other: School. School nurse, nursing home, hospital, broker, insurance company/agent, Cable Company, electric/gas/oil company emergency numbers, pharmacy

Notes:

_____

_____

_____

_____

_____

_____

_____

# Personal/Business Information

This important information will help you establish guidelines for your estate. It will also help you understand the roles of executor, executrix, and guardians; summarize your investments, real estate, and other valuables; and learn what wills and trusts can do for you, your family and your business. This information can also assist your financial adviser, accountant, and attorney for drafting your will or trust.

## Section 1: Personal/Business Information

You
Name _____ SS#/EIN# _____-___-_____
Maiden-name (if applicable) _____
Home address _____
Home-phone_____ Work _____ Fax _____
E-mail_____Work E-mail _____
Occupation _____Employer _____
Employer address _____
Date of birth _____ Citizenship _____

Spouse
Name _____ SS#/
EIN# _____-___-_____
Spouse's maiden name (if applicable) _____
Occupation _____Employer _____
Employer address_____Phone_____Fax _____
Date of birth _____ Citizenship _____

Children

| Name | Address | DOB | SS# | Married/children |
|------|---------|-----|-----|------------------|
| _____ | _____ | _____ | ___-__-___ | _____ |
| _____ | _____ | _____ | ___-__-___ | _____ |
| _____ | _____ | _____ | ___-__-___ | _____ |

Make photocopies of your/spouse's/children's social security numbers and birth certificates, and put them in a safe place.

Parents:

| Name | Address | DOB | State/country of birth* | SS# | Name changes |
|------|---------|-----|-------------------------|-----|--------------|
| _____ | _____ | __/__/____ | _____ | __-__-____ | _____ |
| _____ | _____ | __/__/____ | _____ | __-__-____ | _____ |
| _____ | _____ | __/__/____ | _____ | __-__-____ | _____ |
| _____ | _____ | __/__/____ | _____ | __-__-____ | _____ |

*This will help when establishing a family tree, legacies, and so on.

Grandchildren

| Name | Address | DOB | SS# | Parents |
|------|---------|-----|-----|---------|
| _____ | _____ | __/__/____ | __-__-____ | _____ |
| _____ | _____ | __/__/____ | __-__-____ | _____ |
| _____ | _____ | __/__/____ | __-__-____ | _____ |

**Great-Grandchildren**

| Name | Address | DOB | SS# | Parents |
|------|---------|-----|-----|---------|
| _____ | _____ | __/__/____ | __-__-____ | _____ |
| _____ | _____ | __/__/____ | __-__-____ | _____ |
| _____ | _____ | __/__/____ | __-__-____ | _____ |

*Prior Marriages

You _____

Spouse _____

*Obligations to provide child support, continued life insurance, health insurance, or alimony for the benefit of prior spouse or children?

$_____

| | | |
|---|---|---|
| [3]Living will? | Yes _____ No _____ |
| Existing will? | Yes _____ No _____ |
| Last updated?          Date          _____ | |
| Existing trusts? | Yes _____ No _____ |
| Are the trusts funded? | Yes _____ No _____ |

You need to place the assets in title into the trust, home, broker accounts, bank accounts, and so on. Anything outside the trust goes to probate.

---

[3]  Living will: A will that states whether or not you wish to be kept alive by artificial means if permanently injured or ill.

Inherited assets:

Did you file 706, 1040, or 1041?                                          Yes _____ No _____

Value of inheritance          $ _____

Federal estate taxes paid     $ _____

## Section 2: Assets

| Market value | Joint/individual | Location/acct# | * Corp/FLP/trust |
|---|---|---|---|
| Primary residence | _____ | _____ | _____ |
| Investment real estate | _____ | _____ | _____ |
| Cash | _____ | _____ | _____ |
| Stocks | _____ | _____ | _____ |
| Bonds | _____ | _____ | _____ |
| CDs | _____ | _____ | _____ |
| Managed portfolios | _____ | _____ | _____ |
| Stock options | _____ | _____ | _____ |
| Annuities (variable/fixed) | _____ | _____ | _____ |
| Life insurance cash value | _____ | _____ | _____ |
| Business interests | _____ | _____ | _____ |
| *Managed trusts | _____ | _____ | _____ |
| Automobile | _____ | _____ | _____ |
| Jewelry, art, antiques | _____ | _____ | _____ |
| Other assets | _____ | _____ | _____ |
| Grand total assets | $_____ | | |

*Family estate trusts, investment management trusts, family limited partnerships, charitable remainder trusts, contract trusts, asset protection trusts, special needs trusts*

## Section 3: Debt

| | Balance | Loan # | Lender |
|---|---|---|---|
| Primary residence | _____ | _____ | _____ |
| Investment real estate | _____ | _____ | _____ |
| | _____ | _____ | _____ |
| | _____ | _____ | _____ |
| Business loans | _____ | _____ | _____ |
| Credit cards | _____ | _____ | _____ |
| Automobile(s) | _____ | _____ | _____ |
| | _____ | _____ | _____ |
| Other | _____ | _____ | _____ |

Frank J. Eberhart, CEP®, RFC®

# Section 4: Life Insurance

|  | Policy 1 | Policy 2 | Policy 3 |
|---|---|---|---|
| [4]Type of insurance | _____ | _____ | _____ |
| Owner (you or trust) | _____ | _____ | _____ |
| Face value | _____ | _____ | _____ |
| Cash value | _____ | _____ | _____ |
| Beneficiaries | _____ | _____ | _____ |
| Premiums | _____ | _____ | _____ |
| | | | |
| **Insurance company(s)** | | | |
| Name: | _____ | _____ | _____ |
| Loans | _____ | _____ | _____ |
| Other | _____ | _____ | _____ |
| Total: | _____ | _____ | _____ |

Grand total debt/liabilities:     $ _____

Grand total assets:     $ _____
Minus
Grand total debt/liabilities     −$_____

Net worth     $_____

Life insurance is income tax free, however if it is not placed into an Irrevocable Life Insurance Trust (ILIT) It is taxable at face value for your estate. There are two things to remember about insurance: (1) it is taxable at face value in your estate unless in an ILIT and or you have any incidence of ownership in the policy, and (2) gifting rules apply to transfers of cash values exceeding $14,000 to new owners. Anything over that amount is subject to gift tax laws. If you transfer an existing insurance policy or any asset, you have a 5-year look back for Medicaid to put a claim on those assets, after 5 years Medicaid has no claim to the transferred assets-this is each person, we will discuss later in qualifying for Medicaid on page 24. The IRS can bring back the assets and make it taxable to the estate. This applies to wills and trusts. Check current gifting rules and amounts at www.irs.gov/uac/Form-706

---

[4]  Type of insurance you own: variable, term (10, 15, 20, 30 years), key-man, long-term care, disability, other

## Administration of Your Estate

Here are some definitions & duties with which you should be familiar:

- Executor/Executrix: The person who takes your will to probate, collects the assets, orders appraisals, makes payments, and distributes the estate according to your will. This individual is personally liable for the investments and processes of the estate, be sure you make the executor aware of this fact.

- Trustee: The person or individual to whom the executor entrusts the assets if there are minor children. The executor manages the money until the children reach the attained age. The successor trustee is someone other than you or your spouse. A successor trustee is needed in the event that both husband and wife die. While one or both of you are alive, you are the trustees. Some states hold the trustees liable for any losses in portfolio values; any beneficiary has the right to sue that trustee for the losses. You may consider a corporate trustee for this service.

- Guardian: The person or individual who will take care of your children and make decisions on their behalf until they reach attained age. If you do not make an appointment, the guardian could be the state.

|  | Name | Address | Relationship |
|---|---|---|---|
| Yourself | | | |
| Executor | _____ | _____ | _____ |
| Trustee | _____ | _____ | _____ |
| Children's guardian | _____ | _____ | _____ |
| | | | |
| Spouse | | | |
| Executor | _____ | _____ | _____ |
| Trustee | _____ | _____ | _____ |
| Children's guardian | _____ | _____ | _____ |

Please use the space below to provide any special instructions or requests for the above-mentioned persons in the event of simultaneous deaths.

_____

_____

_____

_____

[5]Power of attorney (POA): for financial and durable power of attorney for health care for each of you. A Power of attorney is necessary for deed transfers, financial decisions, health decisions, a will does not provide for incapacitation for any of these events.

| | |
|---|---|
| You | Yes/No |
| Spouse | Yes/No |
| Life Partner | Yes/No |

## Section 6: Special Needs and Circumstances

You may wish to provide for your parents, children, grandchildren, and yourself.

Long-term health care policies _____ Policy # _____
Special needs trust* _____ Trust tax ID # _____

| Name | Address | Relationship | Date of Birth |
|---|---|---|---|
| _____ | _____ | _____ | __/__/__ |
| _____ | _____ | _____ | __/__/__ |
| _____ | _____ | _____ | __/__/__ |
| _____ | _____ | _____ | __/__/__ |

*Special needs trusts are designed to provide income flow for disabled or handicapped individuals and to make sure that they are protected. These trusts provide protection against creditors.

**There are three types of Special Needs Trusts.**
1. This would be where a family sets up a Trust and funds the Trust with their own assets/money to care for the one with special needs.
2. The second is usually tied to a court action when someone was injured at birth, a car accident or any other type of court action where the Judge awards a settlement. Usually the Judge will want a trust to oversee the finances.
3. The third type is the most difficult (any time the government is involved it becomes more complex) if the individual is receiving Medicare, Medicaid or SSI from the state or federal government. Each plan has specific rules as to what they will pay and the Trust can pay only for the items not covered by the government plan. If the Trustee pays for a benefit provided by the government program, then the government will stop paying for all benefits and it can take up to six months to reinstate the benefits.

---

[5] If you or your spouse becomes incapacitated, the power of attorney allows you or your spouse to make health care and financial decisions for each other. Your will does not cover incapacitation; instead, such power is court appointed. This applies to your business as well as personal; most companies do not have a succession plan in place.

It is important to have a Trustee who has knowledge in the area of Medicaid, Medicare or SSI; one would not want to loose the benefits.

List special needs requirements: (skilled nursing, handicapped, etc.)

_____

_____

_____

_____

**QTIP** (qualified terminal interest property trusts) Are generally used for previous marriages with children to help insure your assets pass to the rightful heirs or beneficiaries. The trust income goes to the surviving spouse (he or she cannot raid corpus, the principal or hard assets unless specified). You can designate an IRA to the QTIP for income to the surviving spouse, this must be done through an independent trustee.

Notes:

# Trusts, Wills, Probate, and Executor Duties

This section includes types of trusts, wills, and definitions with which you should be familiar. Most individuals do not realize that when they die, there are three choices for transfer of wealth:

- By law
- By contract
- By probate

Each state uses either civil or common law. Common law states allows assets to be split after individuals (married or not) have been living together for a certain period of time. Civil law recognizes the individual's private rights. Most states use common law.

Probate is a court-appointed system to oversee the direction and fair distribution of one's last wishes according to his or her will or testamentary trust. Once the assets have passed through probate, which can take six months or more, they receive a step-up in cost basis and are distributed to the claims of beneficiaries. ***Creditors such as Medicaid have a right to property or assets before the heirs do.*** Probate fees vary and can be costly. The executor of the estate is also entitled to fees, most of which is based on the value of the estate.

Testamentary trusts are trusts written inside a will; the will/trust goes to probate then back to the trust-kind of defeats the purpose and can cause other tax problems, Revocable and Amendable Trusts are private (wills are public), the primary benefits of an RLT (revocable living trust) are bypassing probate even though you need to file and pay a probate fee in the county you live in, it does not go to probate and the assets are generally distributed much faster than a will.

## The duties of the executor/executrix include the following:

- Read your will and expedite burial instructions. Meet with the attorney and key family members.
- Safeguard your assets before the official court appointment of executor. The listed executor/executrix of the estate needs to review all insurance, stock/bank portfolios, personal property, and any business interests, and he or she must give notice to all accounts such as banks, credit cards, brokerage houses, insurance companies, etc.
- Petition the court for probate of your will. The executor obtains proof of beneficiaries/heirs, locates witnesses, and petitions for probate of your will. He or she also applies for all court orders in the administration of the estate (such as getting affidavit of domicile, death certificate, copies of the will or trust) and obtains court appointment for executor/executrix status.
- Assemble and inventory all your assets, including all life insurance policies, tax waivers, and cash. In addition, he or she must inventory and appraise all household goods and remove

valuables to a safe deposit; process all claims for amounts due; locate witnesses on any contested claims; arrange supervision of any business interests; collect all securities including interest and dividends; and review and manage all leases, mortgages, taxes, and real estate.

- Procure appraisal of assets and evidence of true value through proper appraisers as of the date of death.

- Administer your estate, which is governed by your will and the local probate law. You need to make estimates of cash needed to pay taxes, legacies, expenses of administration, and net distribution from probate. The executor makes sure business interests are in order including any liquidation or sale, adjusts any incomplete contracts, and evaluates all real estate and securities for sale if specified by your will or needed to raise cash.

- Prepare and pay your income tax for the year before and the year after death. You must make sure no further liability exists.

- Prepare and pay your inheritance and estate tax, and any state death, federal estate, and inheritance taxes due. He or she will handle any waivers or disclaims of property and releasing of property owned in other states, as well as file all forms and pay all taxes due.

- Settle all proper claims and send notices to creditors.

- Distribute your probated estate. You must prepare a detailed report for all receipts and disbursements, and note the date of the final account to all interested parties. After the court settles the account, the executor/executrix distributes any remaining property as directed by the court.

- Obtain final discharge after the final payment and distribution of all claims

**Beneficiaries listed on your 401K, 403(b), Life Insurance, and IRA's override your will.**

You may want to have an attorney handle the probate process, because of the stress involved, the unfamiliarity of the process, and the time it takes (usually six months or more). The attorney or tax adviser can complete the tax returns, most states now require state estate tax filings and payment within 9 months form the date of death of a spouse. Check out fees prior to signing any agreements, including how much he or she charges for filing the taxes.

Most of the information you need can be obtained by or provided to your attorney if you follow my workbook.

## Terms and definitions you should be familiar with:

- *A will* (inter vivos) is a legal document that administers and distributes your assets by the probate process, according to your instructions. The short term to processing your probate claim is around six months; the long term is twenty-four months or longer. It's relatively easy to contest a will, but more difficult to contest a trust. Wills do not provide direction for incapacitation; the executor for financial decisions generally becomes court appointed, which is a real hassle for heirs and beneficiaries. Wills only provide direction on death. A pour-over will pours the assets from the will into an existing trust created before the death of the testor (grantor). A pour-over will goes through the probate process

- **Non-marital** tax exclusion transfers all the assets from your estate to your surviving spouse. It avoids estate taxes, but it is now fully tax-able in the surviving spouse's estate. The Economic Growth and Tax Relief Reconciliation Act of 2001 called for the phase out of the federal estate tax. Although most tax experts expected Congress to change the law before that happened, the estate tax did die in 2010. It was reinstated, however, in 2011. That tax year, estates in excess of $5 million were taxed at 35 percent. For deaths in 2012, the estate tax exemption increased to $5.12 million thanks to inflation. And thanks to the American Taxpayer Relief Act of 2012, or ATRA, which was passed Jan. 1, 2013, the estate tax was made a permanent part of the tax code and the exemption amount automatically indexed for inflation. For the 2013 tax year, the estate tax exclusion amount is $5.25 million. It increases to $5.34 million for 2014. ATRA also increased the tax rate on estates in excess of the exemption amount from 35 percent to 40 percent. The new estate tax law, however, does offer permanent portability between spouses. This allows the surviving spouse the opportunity to take advantage of any unused estate and gift tax exemption left by the first spouse. The portability option must be selected when the estate tax return of the first spouse is filed, even if no federal estate tax is owed. http://www.irs.gov/pub/irs-pdf/i1040tt.pdf for further updates.

## Annual gift tax exclusion

You can give currently $14,000 for 2014 to each person and to as many individuals as you want, without triggering the gift tax; you file Form 706 with your tax return, always check www.irs.gov/uac/Form-706 for any updates. The amount is indexed each year for inflation. In addition to the annual exclusion amounts, you also can give the following without triggering the gift tax:

- Charitable gifts.
- Gifts to a spouse.
- Gifts to a political organization for its use.
- Gifts of educational expenses. These are unlimited as long as you make a direct payment to the educational institution for tuition only. Books, supplies and living expenses do not qualify.
- Gifts of medical expenses. These, too, are unlimited as long as they are paid directly to the medical facility.
- Plus, with the new state estate taxation, you may have to pay taxes over the state's exemption amount in the year of the death of a spouse. Each state has established a table to determine what you would owe, check your state for testate death tax schedules. A better solution,

if your assets exceed the federal unified estate tax credit, may be utilizing an A/B credit shelter trust and a revocable and amendable living trust.

- *A revocable and amendable living trust (RLT)* is a legal entity that holds or manages the assets for an individual. The grantor is the individual transferring the assets to the trust. As a general rule, both spouses are the trustees and the beneficiaries, and they outline the terms of the trust. You should also fund the trust, which consists of titling the assets in the name of the trust (i.e., John Doe revocable and amendable living trust). These assets could include a house, broker accounts, bank accounts, etc. Anything left outside the trust goes to probate. You need to obtain trust tax ID # and use IRS Form 1041, marked grantor trust; this means there are no tax consequences, so taxable income is attributed to the grantor resulting in paying tax on such income go to the grantor. RLTs bypass probate though you still need to file in the county in which you reside and pay the probate fee. The assets inside the trust step up the cost basis on death and also transfer more easily to the surviving spouse, or any beneficiary. In addition, you need to have a durable power of attorney for health and investment directions; A/B credit shelter trusts; a living will, which indicates what to do if you are sick, terminally ill, etc.; and power of attorneys for you and your spouse. Like a will, RLTs have no impact until death.

**Here are examples of what can go into an RLT (revocable amendable living trust):**
- Stocks
- Bonds
- Mutual funds
- Brokerage accounts
- Variable annuities
- Life insurance (taxable at face value unless in an irrevocable life insurance trust or ILIT)
- Art and collectibles
- Personal possessions
- Capital-managed accounts
- Real estate

**Here are examples of what cannot go into an RLT:**
- IRAs
- Pensions
- 401(k) accounts
- 403(b) and other qualified plans

You can make the beneficiary the revocable trust, and the trust can then be distributed to named beneficiaries.

- *A testamentary trust* (inter vivos) is a trust written inside a will. The will goes to probate and then comes back to the trust. Testamentary trusts defeat the purpose of a trust and can cause other taxation or gift tax problems. Always check with your tax adviser or attorney.

- *Joint tenants with rights of survivorship (JTWROS)* means that as-sets automatically pass to the other partner on death. However, the property and assets must pass through probate, and the entire amount is taxable in the surviving spouse's estate for federal estate tax. The exception is that most states have adopted their own state death tax with an exemption amount of $675,000. Anything over this amount is subject to taxation and must be filed in the year of the death. Check with your state to see what the rules are.

- *Tenancy in common* means that each share of ownership passes in accordance with each co-owner's will. Each individual will be responsible for his or her share of taxation and/or gift tax. This can be a disadvantage if you wish to change ownership positions. Getting some-one's name on a title or an asset is easy; getting the person's name off may not be as simple. Secondly, if you become incapacitated (can't function for yourself), financial decisions may become court appointed if you do not have the correct financial and health care proxies established.

- *Unitrusts* pay income to a beneficiary as a fixed annual percentage of the trust assets value. The percentage remains the same for the en-tire term of the trust agreement. Annuity trusts pay a fixed annual amount to a beneficiary for the term

- *Transfer on death (TOD)* accounts are agreements between you and a brokerage or bank to transfer directly to a specified individual. On your death, the firm transfers the assets directly to the designated individual and you avoid probate. The assets receive a step-up in cost basis on the transferred assets. Most accounts require filing an inheritance claim or waiver of any amount over $25,000, if the designated individual is a Class B beneficiary (cousin, aunt, uncle, or nephew). Be sure to have proper health care and financial proxies included with your will or trust. of the trust.

- *Transferring by contract:* Examples of beneficiary contracts are trusts, annuities, life insur-ance policies, IRAs, and 401(k) plans. These products bypass the probate process and are referred to as beneficiary-designated products. Generally they are not subject to a gift tax or capital gains tax. Life insurance is income tax free and also estate tax free if inside a trust. Living probate is where the beneficiary becomes incapacitated at the time of your death. The issuing insurance or annuity companies may want the courts to oversee the supervision of the assets. Intestate is the state of dying without a will. In this case, your estate will go through the probate process and the courts will oversee the process of your financial affairs. This is not something you want to have happen.

- *A/B credit shelter trust* (CST, also known as a family trust or by-pass trust) is a disclaimer trust that splits assets of individuals to take advantage of the current federal estate tax. Currently 5.34 million for 2014 and 40% over the exemption, it must be placed in an irrevocable credit Shelter Trust (A/B Trust). If you do not use the A/B trust, you have only one exemption. A gift tax of 40 percent still applies to anything gifted out of your estate over the $14,000 per person gift exclusion ($14,000 for 2014). It is generally funded at death; the surviving spouse files IRS Form 706 to activate the trust. If you fund the B trust while you're alive, it uses your current gift tax exemption and you are capped at the current federal estate tax exemption which is $5.34 million for 2014 www.irs.gov/uac/Form-706

- **Intestate** is the state of dying without a will. In this case, your state will go through the probate process and the courts will oversee the process of your financial affairs. The reason is without a will, there is no direction. This is not something you want to have happen.

- *An irrevocable* life insurance trust (ILIT) or wealth replacement trust (WLT) places an insurance policy in trust, making the money in-come tax free and estate-tax free. If the policy is written at the same time as the trust is established, there is no 5-year look-back provision for the IRS to bring the money back into the estate. Policies already issued and placed inside a trust require a five-year look-back for estate tax purposes. In addition, crummy letters are required to be sent each year to beneficiaries that gives them the right to withdraw cash; they need to sign and return stating they do not wish to withdraw cash and it must be filed each year. If not, the IRS audits and if no letters they have the right to bring the insurance back into the estate at face value for federal estate taxes.

Notes:

_____

_____

_____

_____

Sample crummy letter that must be sent and returned by each beneficiary each year for life insurance inside an ILIT (irrevocable life insurance trust:

# Specimen "Crummy" Notice Letter

Date:

Dear Trust Beneficiary:

Please be advised that a gift has been made to the _____ Irrevocable Trust on _____ day of _____, 19_____. As a beneficiary of the trust, pursuant to the provisions of Article III, you have the present right to demand from the trust your pro-rata portion of the gift, in the amount of $_____. If you wish to exercise your right of withdrawal, please do so in writing, addressed to the undersigned, within 30 days of receipt of this letter. If you do not wish to exercise your right of withdrawal within this time period, your right to withdraw will expire. If you do not wish to withdraw from this trust, please sign and date the waiver below and return it to me. Beneficiary Waiver of Withdrawal I acknowledge receipt of the notice of withdrawal for the _____ Irrevocable Trust and hereby relinquish irrevocably such withdrawal right as of the date indicated below.

_____          _____

Date                                             Trust Beneficiary


"The answer should be "no", we decline to receive any cash value as this may undo the trust. IRS audits crummy trust letters, if they have not been sent and returned; IRS can void the estate tax free portion of the trust and bring the assets (face value of the insurance policy) into the estate. The life insurance would still remain income tax-free.


*This sample document has been prepared solely for purposes of illustration and is not intended as legal advice. Any third party recipient of this document must be informed that it is intended only for the guidance of the recipient's own counsel, that it may not be appropriate to the recipient's estate or investment plans, and that the actual document which is to be executed by the recipient must be drawn by the recipient's own counsel and must conform to the laws of the jurisdiction where executed. No responsibility, express or implied, is assumed by the author or any Affiliated Companies and its subsidiaries or their agents and employees for the legal, tax or other effects of this sample document.

# Asset Protection Trusts

The asset protection Trust is established to protect the wealth one has earned over the years from Creditors, lawsuits or judgments. Most states with an Asset Protection Law require the assets/ money to be held in trust for three to four years before the credit protection takes place. States (as of today) like Nevada and Ohio have the shortest statutory period, two years, Ohio 1 year. Why set up a trust where the statutory period is three or four years when it can be obtained in two years. In addition under current Nevada law, if the assets are places in an LLC (limited Liability Company), the first 2 million is exempt immediately from creditors and bankruptcy as long as there is no pending actions against the estate, individual or company.

Nevada currently does not have a limit on the total amount or type of assets that can be placed in the trust where as some states limit the dollar amount to $1 million and the type of assets you can place inside the trust. Ohio has emerged as number 3 in the rankings for asset protection trusts.

The rules for an asset protection Trust are:

1.  Assets have to be in the state the trust is written
2.  The Trust must have a Trustee in that State (A person can be their own Trustee if they live in Nevada or use a Trust Company or Bank)
3.  There must be maintained records showing an accounting for the Trust. These records prove when the Trust was set up and the Two-year statutory period (or any) begins to run.
    *   Always ask if there is a state income tax and what is the rate
    *   Is there a corporate or franchise tax
    *   What is the limit for Dynasty trusts
    *   Is there a capital gains tax
    *   Is there estate Tax
    *   What is the privacy protection (like structuring LLC's & LP's to protect the identity of the client

This illustration shows the power of an asset protection trust, it is based on current Nevada Law-check with your state or estate attorney on the laws of your state.

# Estate Tax Exemption Top Estate Tax Rate

Estate and Gift Tax Table: **Form 1040 (Tax Tables), Tax Table and Tax Rate Schedules**:
http://www.irs.gov/pub/irs-pdf/i1040tt.pdf

State Gift, Estate, Inheritance taxes: http://www.house.leg.state.mn.us/hrd/pubs/estatesurv.pdf

2012: $5,120,000 - 35% above the exemption
2013: $5,250,000 - 35% above the exemption
2014: $5,340,000 –40% above the exemption

Gift tax currently $14,000 (per person) for 2014 at 40% over the exemption.
Gift tax for 2013 and 2014: $14,000 and 40% over the exemption.
You file Form 706 for estate and gift tax.
You need to check on current estate, gift tax rates, exemptions www.irs.gov/uac/Form-706

# Book 2: Budgeting

A budget? Who needs a budget? You do-that's who…unlike the government, we actually need to balance our checkbooks. With a budget you can identify spending habits, which will help you to make necessary changes. I have included sections for monthly amounts as well as your actual, and end of year annualized expenses, and income. This allows you to see your total expenses, and your total income to give you your net spendable income. This will help you to adjust your investment and retirement dollar allocations.

Most individuals do not save enough. In reality, the majority of people will rely on social security (good luck with that) as the main source of retirement funding and Medicare as the health care (good luck again). A study by the Department of Human Services found the following for every one hundred people retiring at age sixty-five:

- Twenty-three will need to continue working—this is the reality for people who don't plan properly.
- Seventy-three will rely on others for support.
- Only four people will retire comfortably.

Bear in mind that, on average, a sixty-five-year old has a 50 percent chance of living to age ninety-two; so it is important not to overlook health care costs including Medicare, [6]Medicare MSA Plans, HSA (health savings account), and other costs and coverage's) when planning for retirement.

*I can't imagine being old and broke because I didn't take the time to do this stuff…*

---

[6] www.cms.gov/Medicare/Health-Plans/MSA

# Personal/Business Budget

## Make a copy for each month or excel spread sheet-you can scan into your computer

Current Month _____     Current year: _____

|  | Monthly | Actual | Difference | End of year actual |
|---|---|---|---|---|
| **Mortgage or rent:** | | | | |
| First mortgage or rent | $_____ | _____ | _____ | _____ |
| Second mortgage | _____ | _____ | _____ | _____ |
| Property 2 | _____ | _____ | _____ | _____ |
| Homeowner's insurance | _____ | _____ | _____ | _____ |
| Other | _____ | _____ | _____ | _____ |
| *Subtotal:* | $_____ | _____ | _____ | _____ |
| | | | | |
| **Real estate taxes** | | | | |
| Property 1 | _____ | _____ | _____ | _____ |
| Property 2 | _____ | _____ | | |
| Property 3 | _____ | _____ | _____ | _____ |
| Other | | | | |
| *Subtotal:* | $_____ | _____ | _____ | _____ |
| | | | | |
| Utilities | _____ | _____ | _____ | _____ |
| Gas and electric | _____ | _____ | _____ | _____ |
| Water and garbage | _____ | _____ | _____ | _____ |
| Telephone | _____ | _____ | _____ | _____ |
| Cable TV | _____ | _____ | _____ | _____ |
| Internet/ISP | _____ | _____ | _____ | _____ |
| Other | _____ | _____ | _____ | _____ |
| *Subtotal:* | $_____ | _____ | _____ | _____ |
| | | | | |
| **Insurance premiums** | | | | |
| Life insurance | _____ | _____ | _____ | _____ |
| Life insurance 2 | _____ | _____ | _____ | _____ |
| Life insurance 3 | _____ | _____ | _____ | _____ |
| Disability insurance | _____ | _____ | _____ | _____ |
| Medical | _____ | _____ | _____ | _____ |

Frank J. Eberhart, CEP®, RFC®

|  | Monthly | Actual | Difference | End of year actual |
|---|---|---|---|---|
| Dental | _____ | _____ | _____ | _____ |
| Other | _____ | _____ | _____ | _____ |
| (Long-term care policies, etc.) | | | | |
| *Subtotal:* $ _____ | _____ | _____ | _____ |
| | | | | |
| *Savings/investments* | _____ | _____ | _____ | _____ |
| Bank accounts | _____ | _____ | _____ | _____ |
| Credit union | _____ | _____ | _____ | _____ |
| CDs | _____ | _____ | _____ | _____ |
| Stocks | _____ | _____ | _____ | _____ |
| Bonds | _____ | _____ | _____ | _____ |
| College funds/529 plans | _____ | _____ | _____ | _____ |
| Annuities | _____ | _____ | _____ | _____ |
| Other | _____ | _____ | _____ | _____ |
| *Subtotal* $ _____ | _____ | _____ | _____ |
| | | | | |
| Tuition and books | _____ | _____ | _____ | _____ |
| (Private school, college, etc.) | _____ | _____ | _____ | _____ |
| Lunch | _____ | _____ | _____ | _____ |
| Childcare | _____ | _____ | _____ | _____ |
| (Special needs, day care, etc.) | | | | |
| Other | _____ | _____ | _____ | _____ |
| *Subtotal:* $ _____ | _____ | _____ | _____ |
| | | | | |
| Transportation | | | | |
| Auto payment 1 | _____ | _____ | _____ | _____ |
| Auto payment 2 | _____ | _____ | _____ | _____ |
| Gas | _____ | _____ | _____ | _____ |
| Insurance | _____ | _____ | _____ | _____ |
| Maintenance | _____ | _____ | _____ | _____ |
| Licenses | _____ | _____ | _____ | _____ |
| Registrations | _____ | _____ | _____ | _____ |
| Tolls/parking | _____ | _____ | _____ | _____ |
| Other | _____ | _____ | _____ | _____ |
| *Subtotal:* $ _____ | _____ | _____ | _____ |

|  | Monthly | Actual | Difference | End of year actual |
|---|---|---|---|---|
| *Charge accounts:* | | | | |
| Visa | _____ | _____ | _____ | _____ |
| MasterCard | _____ | _____ | _____ | _____ |
| American Express | _____ | _____ | _____ | _____ |
| Discover Card | _____ | _____ | _____ | _____ |
| Other | _____ | _____ | _____ | _____ |
| *Subtotal:* | $_____ | _____ | _____ | _____ |
| | | | | |
| *Loan payments* | | | | |
| Loan 1 | _____ | _____ | _____ | _____ |
| Loan 2 | _____ | _____ | _____ | _____ |
| Other | _____ | _____ | _____ | _____ |
| *Subtotal:* | $_____ | _____ | _____ | _____ |
| | | | | |
| Food | _____ | _____ | _____ | _____ |
| Clothing | _____ | _____ | _____ | _____ |
| Other | _____ | _____ | _____ | _____ |
| Travel/vacation | _____ | _____ | _____ | _____ |
| Dining | _____ | _____ | _____ | _____ |
| Dues/subscriptions | _____ | _____ | _____ | _____ |
| Charitable gifts | _____ | _____ | _____ | _____ |
| Other | _____ | _____ | _____ | _____ |
| *Subtotal:* | $_____ | _____ | _____ | _____ |
| | | | | |
| **Total expenses** | $_____ | _____ | _____ | _____ |

| *Income:* | Monthly | Actual | Difference | End of year actual |
|---|---|---|---|---|
| Gross salary 1 | _____ | _____ | _____ | _____ |
| Gross salary 2 | _____ | _____ | _____ | _____ |
| 1099 Income | _____ | _____ | _____ | _____ |
| Rental income | _____ | _____ | _____ | _____ |
| Dividends | _____ | _____ | _____ | _____ |
| Interest | _____ | _____ | _____ | _____ |
| Capital gains | _____ | _____ | _____ | _____ |
| Commissions | _____ | _____ | _____ | _____ |
| Bonus | _____ | _____ | _____ | _____ |
| Other | _____ | _____ | _____ | _____ |
| *Gross income* | $_____ | _____ | _____ | _____ |

|  | Monthly | Actual | Difference | End of year actual |
|---|---|---|---|---|
| *Reductions* | | | | |
| Federal taxes | _____ | _____ | _____ | _____ |
| State/local taxes | _____ | _____ | _____ | _____ |
| Social security | _____ | _____ | _____ | _____ |
| Medicare tax | _____ | _____ | _____ | _____ |
| Medicaid tax | _____ | _____ | _____ | _____ |
| 401(k)/403(b | _____ | _____ | _____ | _____ |
| Other | _____ | _____ | _____ | _____ |
| | | | | |
| **Net Income:** | $_____ | _____ | _____ | _____ |
| | | | | |
| Total net income | $_____ | _____ | _____ | _____ |
| Minus | | | | |
| Total expenses | $_____ | _____ | _____ | _____ |
| | | | | |
| Net cash for savings | $_____ | _____ | _____ | _____ |
| **& Retirement** | | | | |

Note: Make a copy for each month, or put this on an excel spreadsheet. By comparing your estimated monthly budget vs. actual monthly and end of year budget you can make adjustments as needed.

Best Advice I can give for 529 Plans: www.savingforcollege.com
For Financial Aid: www.findaid.org

I think it is just as important to understand what you <u>owe</u> as it is to understand what you <u>own</u> and where it is.

# Long-Term Care Policies/Medicare/Medicaid

As we grow older (only around 35% of baby boomers have long term care policies), medical expenses and prescription medication generally increase. Several areas we will explore are long-term care policies, Medicare, and Medicaid programs. Long-term health care policies are designed to supplement health and living benefits as we get older. You have several choices: buy a long-term health care policy, pay for nursing home or assisted living out of your pocket (note that each state has different costs for services—New Jersey can run $90,000 a year or more), or give away your assets and go on Medicaid. Long-term care polices provide a daily dollar rate for services needed. You can design your own benefit amount and any periods of waiting before the benefit goes into effect. So if you choose a 90-day waiting period, the first 90 days are out of your pocket, then your daily dollar amount starts paying for your care facility.

Things you should consider when researching a policy are as follows:

- Does the policy provide for in-home care, nursing home, or assisted living? The national average for nursing home care exceeds $54,000 per year. Assisted living is very expensive and generally requires large up-front fees to join with high monthly maintenance thereafter. Check all of this out prior to buying any policy-you need to make sure what you buy is going to cover what you get.
- What coverage such as prescription drugs, around-the-clock nursing care, and rent, is your premium quote covering? Is the coverage 100 percent or 80 percent?
- Does the policy contain a waiver of premium if you are confined to a nursing home or other care facility?
- What is the policy period for which you are being quoted? Is it three years, five years, ten years, or lifetime? If the policy is for a set number of years, you will run out of coverage at the end of the stated contract period. You then must pay for your care out of pocket.
- Is the policy portable? If you move to another state or facility, can you take the benefit with you?
- If you are younger and buy a long-term care policy, it may be beneficial to purchase a compounding benefit rate.
- Does it provide spousal discounts?
- Does it cover Alzheimer's, Parkinson's, or dementia?
- Check to see if your policy is tax deductible.
- **Premiums are not guaranteed and may go up over time.**
- Many corporations are now providing long-term care polices as a benefit.

Some newer annuities are providing nursing home riders in the policies

## Medicare and Medicaid

- Medicare (started in 1966) only covers nursing home care for a maximum of one hundred days, and only after an immediate hospital stay of four days. It does not provide for in-home nursing, or assisted living. It is a medical and drug prescription program sponsored by the government which goes into effect as primary medical coverage at age sixty-five. See www.medicare.gov. Medicare MSA Plans: www.cms.gov/medicare/health-plans/msa

- Medicaid is a joint federal-state health insurance program designed for transferring or selling your assets to pay for your nursing home care—not a good choice, but in some cases necessary. Beware of look-back provisions transferring assets (60 months for regular transfers (wills) and sixty months for trusts). After the look-back, Medicaid has no claim on the transferred assets. The IRS might have a claim if the assets were not filed under gift tax on form 706 or not sold at 70 percent of fair market value. You can use IRS form 706 (gift tax) exemption to transfer assets to avoid look-back provisions (you have currently $14,000 per year per person to anybody, and 1 million life time (check with www.irs.gov/uac/Form-706 for any changes to the gift tax exemption) which can be used anytime for real estate, investments, art work, etc.).

Keep in mind that IRS (not just Medicaid) has a claim for any assets transferred improperly above the exemption amount in any year and can impose fines and penalties from the date of transfer and charge the gift tax rate currently at 40%.

## Medicaid rules:

- Look back is 5 years for wills and trusts for assets transferred out of you or your spouse's names. It is generally unlimited transferring spouse to spouse i.e., houses, bank accounts, etc. After 5 years Medicaid has no claim against any of the assets transferred, HOWEVER-if you only transfer one spouse to the other, it only covers that spouse, the other spouse is now locked in and not able to transfer any assets out of their name for any purpose, it is considered an improper transfer of assets (or Medicaid FRAUD) and will result in a penalty period equal to any amount transferred out or any assets that are above the QUALIFYING asset level currently at around $115,000 (check your state or current amounts at www.hcfa.gov . in addition, if the other spouse goes to a nursing home, then all assets could be lost to Medicaid NOT the beneficiaries
- Example: If Jane Doe has $226,000 in assets-$115,000 allowable= $111,000 over. Divide that number by $6414 (average monthly cost of a nursing home) it would equal around 17 months that she would be ineligible for Medicaid services.

- Make sure you have transferred all assets <u>before you apply for Medicaid</u>, and if you want exemptions YOU BOTH need to transfer assets irrevocably out of your estate.
- Spend down of asserts, you are allowed approximately $1500 month in your account.
- Rules of the halves, if only individual enters a nursing home, ½ of the assets are transferred or Medicaid entitled, the other half allows the other spouse to remain in the home, and maintain assets. If both enter the nursing home under Medicaid, then Medicaid has claim to all assets.
- Annuities and life insurance. You can assign a portion of your life insurance policy to a funeral home to pay for any and all funeral expenses. Medicaid can only claim the balance if any for the policy. annuities and planning, annuities must be made irrevocable, the state must be named beneficiary up to the amount of Medicaid paid on the annuitants behalf.
- Watch out for "consultants" that claim they can help you beat the system or bend the rules-any questions or concerns call: 1-800-633-4227 or TTY/TDD 1-877-486-2048 or visit any of the web sites on the next page.
- * You can assign the amount of funeral costs from your life insurance policy to the funeral home and exclude that amount from Medicaid.

## Probate is one of the biggest collectors for Medicaid

For more information, go to Medicaid online at

www.hcfa.gov or
**www.medicaid.gov**
**www.cms.gov**

The following Web sites can provide more specific information on elderly care:

National Library of Medicine at
www.nlm.nih.gov/medline/nursinghomes.html
U.S. Department of Health at
www.medicare.gov/nhcompare/home.asp
www.cms.gov/medicare/health-plans/msa
To apply for: Social security benefits:
www.socialsecurity.gov/applyforbenefits
Or call 1-800-772-1213
Medicare: www.medicare.gov

# Retirement Budget

## The goal is to live <u>off</u> your assets...<u>not</u> on them

We have discussed your net cash flow and budget while working; now let's examine your desired level of living following retirement. To retire in a comfortable lifestyle takes preparation, good investment strategies, organization, commitment, discipline, review, changes when needed, and A BUDGET.

Most individuals think that once they retire, they no longer need to invest. This couldn't be farther from reality. For every dollar you take out, you will probably need to replace it with a minimum of $2. You need to be aware of withdrawal rates (see impact of withdrawal rates below) and inflation and how they impact your money. For example, look at 3 percent inflation on $1 over the last thirty years. You need around $2.50 to equal that one dollar.

## Estimated Expenses Needed for Retirement

| | Monthly | Annually |
|---|---|---|
| Mortgage | | |
| Property taxes | | |
| Gas/maintenance/registrations | | |
| Utilities | | |
| Food | | |
| Telephone/cell phones | | |
| Cable | | |
| Credit cards | | |
| Life Insurance premiums | | |
| *LTC | | |
| Medicare Premiums | | |
| Medicare part A and B | | |
| Vacation home(s) | | |
| Travel/vacations planned | | |
| Medical premiums | | |
| **HSA account | | |
| Taxes (quarterly estimates) | | |
| All other expenses | | |
| | | |
| *Expenses total* | $_____ | $_____ |

*Long-term health care insurance (LTC).

Go to www.medicare.gov and www.ssa.gov for social security and to www.irs.gov . These sites can provide calculators to help with cost estimates.

**A health savings account is tax free for health care; you pay ordinary income for any other purpose. www.opm.gov in search type in HSA for Medicare: www.cms.gov/medicare/health-plans/msa

The IRS requires a quarterly tax payment based on estimated passive income after retirement. Check with your accountant or tax adviser for more details.

| Estimated Income | Monthly | Annual |
|---|---|---|
| Pension's | _____ | _____ |
| Social security | _____ | _____ |
| Stocks/bonds/CDs | _____ | _____ |
| Annuities | _____ | _____ |
| Ira's | _____ | _____ |
| Rental property income | _____ | _____ |
| All other income | _____ | _____ |
| | | |
| **Income total** | $_____ | $_____ |
| | | |
| Minus expenses | $_____ | $_____ |
| | | |
| *Total money available*: | $_____ | $_____ |

# The Impact of Withdrawal Rates on Your Money

## Withdrawal rates and the number of years expected to last

Based on historical data, utilizing a balanced portfolio of 50 percent stocks, 40 percent bonds, and 10 percent cash or equivalents and adjusted for inflation. These are only hypothetical's, and returns will vary based on your investment selection. This information is general and intended for educational purposes only.

**If you retire at 65**

Withdraw:

| | | |
|---|---|---|
| 10% | money will last 11 years to age 76 |
| 9% | money will last 13 years to age 78 |
| 8% | money will last 15 years to age 80 |
| 7% | money will last 18 years to age 83 |
| 6% | money will last 21 years to age 86 |
| 5% | money will last 27 years to age 92 |
| 4% | money will last 33 years to age 98 |

Beneficiaries listed on your 401K, 403(b), Life Insurance, and IRA's override your will.
Make sure they all match

Annuities can offer important benefits such as guaranteed death benefits, guaranteed income, portfolio selection based on risk, and survivorship benefits. Make sure you check out all expenses and risks associate with the purchase of an annuity such as CDSC charges (declining sales charge, withdrawal limitations, and make sure you are not losing your guaranteed death benefit, the amount you transfer from an old annuity becomes your new death benefit. Be careful of "indexed annuities" for more information go to: www.sec.gov/answers/annuity.htm SEC Web page for annuities

*When I retire I want to live a better life style than when I worked*

# How Much Life Insurance Do You Need?

The primary purpose for life insurance is the death benefit that it provides. Typically, you need to pass a physical to qualify for life insurance, and you must have an insurable interest in the party being insured. The goal is to cover living expenses for your surviving spouse, pay for final expenses, and pay for any federal and state estate taxes due. Life insurance should not act as a retirement plan. The cost of insurance increases over time and can erode any cash value you may think that you are accumulating. If you do accumulate excess cash flow and start taking out annual withdrawals, and the policy lapses because of failure to make premium payments on the loans, you could face a tax bill on the investment gain you made. The formula would be the following:

$$\text{Loans-Premiums Paid} = \text{Portfolio Gain} \times \text{Your Tax Bracket}$$

Make sure the life agent doesn't try to sell you a policy with distorted values for the projections of returns. The higher the return, the lower your premium will be. The problem is that if you run 10 percent or more and it does not perform, you could find yourself adding additional premiums in later years.

## Basic types and purpose of life insurance

When you buy a life insurance policy, the face value of the policy is income tax free (not estate tax free) to your beneficiaries if the policy is held in your name, you have incidence of ownership,[7] or the estate is named as the beneficiary. However, it will be taxable at the face value of the estate; the interest is also taxable if not in an irrevocable life insurance trust for federal estate tax purposes. The ILIT (irrevocable life insurance trust) is a separate trust that owns the life insurance policy for the benefit of the named beneficiaries. On death, the proceeds are income tax free and estate tax free. You cannot have any incidence of ownership, and you must send out the Crummy letters (each year, if the IRS audits the trust, and you not sent out and received back the crummy notices, they can void the trust and tax it in the estate at face value) for the IRS to each named beneficiary, giving him or her the right to withdraw cash values. If anyone does withdraw cash, the withdrawal could void the trust. Further, any existing policies placed in an ILIT will carry a five-year look-back provision and must use the annual gifting provision allowed by the IRS, which is currently $14,000 per year per beneficiary.

---

[7] Incidence of ownership means the power to change beneficiaries, borrow against cash values, surrender the policy, or pay premiums directly.

Frank J. Eberhart, CEP®, RFC®

- With variable universal life (VUL), you have investment options to increase cash values to help offset premiums.
- Universal life (UL) is a variation of whole life; it allows you to adjust your premiums and death benefit up or down.
- Whole life combines a death benefit and accumulates cash value. The cash is a fixed amount of interest applied to your fixed premium for the life of the contract.
- Second-to-die policies are used primarily in trusts. Nothing happens when the first spouse dies, but on the second death, the insurance is collected. These policies are usually less expensive.
- Term polices have a fixed face value for a specified period of time: five, ten, fifteen, twenty, or thirty years. They are the least expensive and have no accumulation of cash.

> However, some companies offer a return of premium (ROP) at the end of the specified time. If you do not die you get all your premiums back or can opt for paid up insurance, generally these policies are 25-40% higher in premiums.

- Key-man or buy-sell agreements are generally term insurance. You are buying insurance if you need to replace a key person or purchase another person's interest in the event of death.

You must have an insurable interest to obtain life insurance on another person.

## Life Insurance Calculator

| | |
|---|---|
| Annual income needed for surviving spouse | $_____ |
| Social security benefits | $_____ |
| Interest, dividends, pensions, other income | $_____ |
| Total income (surviving spouse) | $_____ |
| Annual expenses | $_____ |
| (summarized to include mortgage, college costs, auto, food, utilities, etc.; take this from budget worksheet) | |
| Credit card and other debt | $_____ |
| *Final expenses (funeral costs) | $_____ |
| | |
| *Total expenses* | $_____ |
| Total expenses × life expectancy of surviving spouse | $_____ |
| Total income minus expenses | $_____ |
| Liquid assets to pay off debt | $_____ |
| (stocks, bonds, mutual funds) | |

Life insurance on yourself                        $_____
Total liquid assets                               $_____

Shortfall/surplus                                 $_____

You should evaluate your estate with a financial advisor, attorney, or tax adviser to determine any federal or state death taxes that may be due, and add in the additional amount to cover those costs.

These are guidelines that depend on how much life insurance you can afford. To help determine the cost of life insurance (and long-term care insurance), go to www.lifehappens.org

---

\* **You can assign the amount of funeral costs from your life insurance policy to the funeral home and exclude that amount from Medicaid.**

---

# Book 3: Investments

## What type of investor are you?

In an interesting survey recently conducted it found men enrolled more than women in company retirement programs, men were more aggressive and monitored their investments more and state they can do it themselves, women were more inclined to seek an advisor

**So what type of investor are you? Growth or value? Fundamental? Technical?**

- *Value investors* generally focus on buying stocks that appear to be bargains relative to the company's net worth and low P/E ratios. Some circumstances that may make a stock a value buy include: companies that are trading below intrinsic value because of recent competition or management changes, or an industry that is currently out of favor with investors.
- *Growth investors* like companies that are growing quickly, newer companies, and emerging industries. They have greater potential for quick stock appreciation, higher earnings per share (EPS), and, of course, higher risk.
- *Contrarian investors* are value investors to the limit. They believe the time to buy is when no one else wants to, or they focus on stocks or industries that are temporarily out of favor.

**There are two basic types of investment research: fundamental and technical.**

- *Fundamental investors* analyze data about the company and operations. Fundamental analysts evaluate figures and try to assess the company's prospects and determine what the shares may be worth after evaluating the company's potential. Buy-and-hold investors generally focus on fundamental data.
- *Technical investors* focus on the company's stock price rather than its operations. They prefer to identify trading patterns on charts that reflect price history and trading volume for a particular stock. The technical analyst helps them identify stocks that are trending higher or lower and trends in the market as a whole. A combination of fundamental and technical analysis, along with diversification of growth and value, can give you a balance in your investment portfolios. Independent asset management (IAM) accounts, sometimes referred to as WRAP fee from 1–3 percent (whatever you negotiate) for mutual funds, stocks, and bonds. The advantage is that the flat fee is generally all you pay. You buy mutual funds at net asset value (NAV), which are Class A shares without the sales load, and pay no commissions on stock trades. There is usually a cap on how many trades per year you're allowed to avoid day traders and no or low markup on bonds, which produces higher yields. It can be a real advantage for mutual funds to avoid all the hidden costs (except 12b-1 fees

that companies charge for advertising) that could raise the total cost of ownership above 3 percent. Commissions on stocks in and out (buy and sell) can be costly and can directly affect your profit. If you prefer to pay commission for each trade, try to keep the commission to 2 percent or less for your stock trades—and compare bond quotes and charges for front-end load mutual funds. You need to look at overall costs in mutual funds. I prefer a flat-fee program because you control your cost, eliminate commissions on security trades, and generally deduct the fee when filing taxes. It also takes the "trading" or "churning" out of the picture. I have always thought that the turnover by brokers for commissions in investments benefited them more than it did the client-no trades, no commissions, no payday! The fee is something you never see in mutual funds because it's taken out of fund performance, and bonds already contain a mark-up. With managed money or WRAP account programs, you see the fee up front every quarter-even though it is generally less than that of traditional funds (you buy mutual funds at NAV, bonds with little or no mark-up, and no commissions on stock trades). You need to get over the psychological barrier of the fee dilemma; generally it is a tax deduction as well.

If you allow discretionary trading (giving someone else the authority to trade on your behalf without asking you), make sure you do a complete background check. See if the person is registered with the FINRA (formerly the NASD), see www.finra.com, and SEC, www.sec.gov If trading futures, make sure the person is registered with the Commodity Futures Trading Commission. Go to www.nfa.futures.org or www.cftc.gov or call1-800-621-3570.

**Now let's look at what makes you select any type of investment (or purchase):**

# Risk and Reward Questionnaire

The importance of finding your financial DNA (risk tolerance) has become more evident over the last few years of market and portfolio declines. Understanding what influences you to buy or sell can help you keep your investment strategy in line with your tolerance for actual losses. Although losing10 percent in your portfolio doesn't sound like a lot, consider that you need about 25 percent the following year to break even. When you fill out the questionnaire on the next page, be honest and don't cheat yourself.

What is your current allocation of investments?

| | | | |
|---|---|---|---|
| Cash | _____% | Stock | _____% |
| Fixed income | _____% | Annuities | _____% |
| CDs | _____% | International | _____% |
| Real estate | _____% | Other | _____% |

What is your involvement with the decision-making process of your investments?

_____

What is your experience with investments?

Stocks____ Bonds____ Mutual funds____

Options____ Annuities____ CDs_____ REITs[8]____

To find out where your risk and reward tolerances lie, assign each of the following questions a score. Numbering is as follows:

1. Strongly disagree
2. Slightly disagree
3. Neutral
4. Slightly agree
5. Strongly agree

_____ I am willing to accept greater price volatility in return for potentially higher long-term gains.

_____ Generating a return that offsets the effect of inflation is very important to me.

_____ I do not need current income from my investments.

_____ My investment goals are long term (greater than seven years).

_____ I am generally a risk taker.

---

[8] Real estate investment trust

_____ I am generally not a risk taker.

_____ I am willing to bear an above-average level of risk and can accept years of negative returns.

_____ I do not need to convert my investments into cash; I have enough liquid assets to meet my expenses.

_____ If I invested $10,000 in a long-term investment six months ago and its current value is now $8,500, I would probably keep the investment.

Total your score. The higher the number, the more risk you are willing to take.

Let's look at the following risk allocation categories.

- *Conservative*: Safety of principal is the main objective and minimal risk is involved.

- *Conservative to moderate*: The primary objective is safety of principal, but the secondary objective is growth of capital.

- *Moderate*: Growth of capital and safety of principal are both important. Moderate risk is acceptable to increase capital appreciation.

- *Moderate to aggressive*: The primary objective is growth of capital and a secondary goal is safety of principal. A fair amount of risk is acceptable to take advantage of greater growth opportunities.

- *Aggressive*: The primary objective is growth of capital. High risk is acceptable in seeking superior returns.

Generally, most people fall into a moderate investment attitude (a score of around a three to four in the above test). Balanced portfolios may be a better idea for these individuals. Have your financial adviser show you numbers that will better illustrate the asset allocation. You can find many modules for this, along with the ratings on most mutual funds, at Web sites such as www.morningstar.com or www.personalfund.com. For example, if your total score from the questions above is 17–22, you might consider a portfolio balance of 30 percent money market, 30 percent fixed income, and 40 percent equities. If your score is 29–34, you might consider 10 percent cash, 10 percent fixed income, and 80 percent equities. You need to match your goals to your investment risk, available investable income (from the budget worksheet), and time frame. Note: These examples are for educational purposes only and are not intended for investment advice. Check with your financial adviser or other financial professional for a more accurate measurement of your risk tolerances. In addition, always read a prospectus before investing. Remember that all investments have some form or element of risk-CDs may not keep up with inflation, stocks may lose value, bonds can default, and so on. Common sense, organization, and research, and true diversification are your best protections for safeguarding your money and investments. Know what you are buying and the costs and risks associated with them. If you are uncomfortable or don't understand what you are investing or getting into, *don't invest.* Remember the old saying: if it sounds too good to be true, it probably is. Always ask questions.

Rule of 72 is a rule of thumb to calculate how long it will take to double your money, if your money is earning 6%, divide 6 into $72 = 12$ years. Substitute any percentage (%) into the 72 to see how long it will take.

# Here is some really boring (but important information):

## Who Regulates This Stuff?

The Securities Exchange Commission (SEC) regulates mutual funds under the Investment Act of 1940, the Securities Act of 1933, and the Securities Exchange Act of 1934. These laws state that mutual funds must be sold with a prospectus that outlines commissions and explains fees, investment objectives, and expenses. I strongly recommend reading the prospectus or having someone explain it to you. There is no easy method for understanding the complexities of mutual funds. Most managers never disclose what overlap exists, what is good for taxable or nontaxable accounts, or what is the internal rate of return to the investor. You can request what the after-tax returns are; managers are required to disclose this, and you can calculate the internal rate using the formula in step 8a. Always look at the holdings inside the funds you own to help avoid overlap and add to true diversification.

The operation of a mutual fund consists of a board of directors/trustees, officers, attorneys, an independent public accountant, custodian, administrator, transfer agent, principal underwriter, investment adviser—and you, the shareholder. Almost all funds are all externally managed; they generally have no employees and hire outside investment managers, broker-dealers, and banks.

Most funds are open-ended, which means that they pay capital gains or losses at the end of each year and continually issue new shares that can be purchased or redeemed at any time-like a stock for current end-of-day value or NAV. The value is the closing price for each trading day; it is derived by taking its total value, subtracting expenses, and dividing by the total number of shares outstanding.

A closed-end fund may issue stocks or bonds and trades on an exchange or purchased from a broker. The share price is negotiated at the end of each day, based on supply and demand or market conditions. You buy or sell and receive market price at the time of the sale.

*Investor note*: Most companies no longer offer pension plans, so it is up to you to save for your retirement. Most of your contributions, if you participate, will be to your 401(k), IRA, annuities, or other qualified plans that your employer offers.

**Many mutual fund** companies now offer balanced portfolios with a choice of the asset allocation classes all in one account such as large-cap value, small/mid-cap, growth, income, bonds, and various styles like aggressive, moderate, conservative, etc. The advantages of this plan generally include the daily rebalancing and reallocating of funds or cash in your portfolio. This takes the guesswork out of what and when to buy or sell, which could be advantageous for the less-experienced investor-and, in many cases, the experienced investor as well.

By law, mutual funds must pass on income and capital gains from investments to the shareholders in both qualified and nonqualified plans. In nonqualified mutual funds, if you sell before one year, the sale is considered a short-term capital gain and is taxed at your current income tax rate.

Frank J. Eberhart, CEP®, RFC®

Selling after one year or longer is a long-term capital gain, currently at 15 percent of your profit. The new NAV, after the fund has declared its end-of-year capital gain distribution, is decreased by that capital gains distribution. In other words, if you pay $20 per share and the capital gain is $5, your new value, or NAV, is $15. You buy more shares at the new NAV and hope for appreciation in the coming year. Your other option is to take the capital gain as a cash distribution and reinvest it in other funds. If your current mutual funds are performing well, why sell? By doing this, you are, in essence, rebalancing your portfolio.

**Closed-end funds**, you are issued a 1099B form. In a closed-end fund, the fund pays tax on the gains at the corporate tax rate and reinvests the proceeds back into the fund versus distributing the long-term gains to the shareholders. If this occurs, you must file a separate Form 2439, Notice to Shareholders of Long-Term Capital Gains. You report this on line 64, page 2, of your 1040. Your cost basis is increased by the difference between long-term capital gains not distributed and the taxes paid by the fund.

Always check the top holdings inside the fund. You want to avoid overlap (the same stocks) by choosing different funds and strategies to diversify.

"Rebalancing" and "asset allocation" have been buzzwords for the last few years. In reality, rebalancing quarterly, semiannually, and annually have not been as successful as actively rebalancing daily or monthly and reallocating profits to other areas for further diversification.

The example below assumes you started with a $10,000 investment and watch it over a five-year period:[9]

| | |
|---|---|
| Rebalanced quarterly: | $9,609 |
| No rebalancing: | $9,900 |
| Benchmark S&P 500, LBAB (Lehman bond index) | $11,090 |
| Rebalanced actively (daily or monthly) | $12,020 |

Dollar-cost averaging uses the strategy of investing a fixed dollar amount at regular intervals—every two weeks, monthly, or quarterly. This takes advantage of market fluctuations over time and reduces the average share price you pay.

**TIP**: If you want additional rebalancing, instead of re-investing dividends back into stock or mutual funds, take the cash and invest in something else or spend it. If you have high yield or income funds, you also might want to take the cash and invest somewhere else for further diversification. One of the problems I find with re-investing stock dividends is that you end up with a lot of odd lot or fractional shares (or like GM, AIG, etc. where you lost everything) that are hard to get rid of; one advantage to re-investing stock dividends is that it increases your cost basis for a future sale.

---

[9] Source: Based on a Thompson Financial report using a $10,000 investment at NAV on 12/31/99 through 12/31/2004 and no withdrawals.

## The Basics: Classification of Funds Understand the difference:

- *Load funds* charge up-front sales commissions, usually a class A share. This can be as high as 8.75 percent, plus your management fees, trading costs, distribution fees, redemption fees, taxes, etc. Class A shares generally offer lower fund fees versus C shares or B shares.

- *No-load funds* have no up-front sales commissions, but they still have trading costs, manager's fees, 12b-1 fees, distribution costs, redemption costs, and taxes.

- *Class A shares* generally have the lowest expense ratios, but you pay an up-front fee ranging from around 3.5–8.75 percent. No charges are incurred to sell the fund.

- *Class B shares* are no-load up front (no sales commission), but they have CDSC on the back end if you sell them. The charges can range as high as 6 percent and decline each year, up to six years. Plus you have 12b-1 fees, which are .25 percent. At the end of the CDSC, the B shares convert to A shares.

- *Class C shares* are no-load and generally have higher administrative charges. They carry a one-year CDSC charge of 1 percent if sold before one year is up.

- *Institutional funds* include class D and I. They are typically sold in defined contribution plans and brokerage WRAP account programs, in which a flat fee is charged for the funds.

## Types of Funds We See Most Often

Most funds are benchmarked against an unmanaged index-a passive index like the S&P 500. Here are some examples of common funds:

- *Large-cap growth funds* generally invest in companies with long-term earnings that are consistent and expect to grow significantly over time. They generally pay no or low dividends. The unmanaged index is the S&P 500.

- *Large-cap value funds* look for long-term growth from companies that are considered undervalued compared with an unmanaged stock index (passive). They generally have a below-average price-to-earnings (P/E) ratio. Normally these funds have an average price-to-earnings ratio, are benchmarked with the S&P Mid-Cap 400 Index, and pay higher dividends.

- *Mid-cap growth funds* generally have an above-average price-to-earnings ratio and are expected to grow faster than an unmanaged stock index. The Lipper Mid-Cap Growth Index is the unmanaged benchmark.

- *Small-and mid-cap value funds* are generally construed as undervalued, have a lower P/E ratio, and seek long-term moderate growth. The Russell 2500 Value Index is the unmanaged benchmark.

- *Small-cap growth funds* are weighted against the S&P Small Cap 600 Index, generally have above-average P/E ratios, and are expected to grow considerably faster than an unmanaged stock index. They also can be very volatile.

- *S&P 500 Index A* is a passively managed index that benchmarks the performance of the S&P 500 on a reinvested basis. The stocks will rise and fall with the market, so volatility becomes an issue.

- *Life cycle funds* are fairly new. They invest more aggressively when you are younger, and as you get older, they start to invest more conservatively and eventually invest for income.

- *Balanced funds* generally have a mix of growth and dividend paying value stocks and higher-quality bonds. Balanced funds provide a more stable (less volatile) portfolio; the bonds help balance out and support income and reduce volatility. The S&P 500 Index is the general benchmark.

- *International value funds* generally invest in large capitalized corporations with a record of stable earnings and consistent dividend payments.

- *Emerging market funds* target securities with very high return potential and carry very high volatility. They deal with countries that are in an emerging growth stage of development. Generally, they are pure growth, and risk occurs if they don't develop, have unstable governments, and so on. They are benchmarked with the Lipper Small-Cap Growth Funds and the Russell 2000 Growth Index.

- *Developing market funds* seek long-term, worldwide growth from companies that will benefit from current economic themes and new technology. They usually have established, stable governments and great potential to develop trade with other countries, but they can be risky and volatile. They are weighted against the MSCI (Morgan Stanley Emerging Market Index).

- *Income funds* try to provide a steady stream of income from fixed investments and higher-paying stock dividends. The target is around 6 percent. The Lipper Income Fund Index is the unmanaged benchmark.

- *Bond funds* invest in various investment-grade corporate bonds as well as government bonds. They are used primarily to help diversify portfolios outside the equities market, with expected average yields of around 5–6 percent. The primary index is the Lipper Intermediate Investment Grade Debt Funds Index.

- *Growth and income funds* generally balance between stocks and bonds and try for a return of 7 percent or greater. The Lipper Income Funds Index is the unmanaged benchmark.

- *Floating rate funds* seek low volatility with high returns. They invest in senior-secured floating-rate loans made to U.S. corporations by larger domestic banks and are designed to keep up with current interest rates. They generally have a shorter duration (time frame to maturity) of three to five years. The Lipper Loan Participation Fund Index is the passive unmanaged benchmark.

- *Municipal bond funds* invest in higher-grade municipalities to generate federal tax-free income. Most states will exempt state interest if you live in the state in which you purchase the bonds. Beware of the alternative minimum tax (AMT) inside the bond funds-AMT can run 25 percent or more. The Lipper High Yield Muni Debt Fund Index is the unmanaged benchmark.

- *High-yield bond funds* offer higher returns and are issued by companies with poor credit ratings or poor credit histories. They are issued to raise capital (debt offerings versus issuing new stock) and pay higher yields than investment-grade securities. The risk is default. Benchmarks are the Lipper High Current Yield Fund and the *S&P 500*

*ETF's and Closed End Funds are now available in "baskets". This allows you to purchase many areas of investment strategies for both income and alternatives while minimizing risk. Generally, share purchases are less as you buy many types of various investment selections in one basket.*

*Notes:*

_____

_____

_____

_____

_____

# Understanding Mutual Funds-Closed End Funds-ETF's (exchange traded funds), Hedge Funds, Bonds, REIT's, Options, 1031 exchanges, Annuities

- *ETF's* or exchange-traded funds started on the American Stock Exchange in 1993 and had around 600 funds, now 19 years later in the thousands. Everybody from money managers, multi sector portfolios, individuals have moved more towards ETF's and out of mutual funds. Why? It's about liquidity, cost, efficiency. With and ETF you can drill down into very specific sectors, like gold, oil, dividend and income, bonds, target date funds etc.. They trade like stocks (if the price is $45 a share and you sell it, you get the traded price-unlike a mutual fund you don't know what you paid for the mutual fund until the end of the day when it settles its NAV-net asset value) on the open market and generally carry lower commissions, and can be bought on margin or borrowed money, or sold short-a sale of a security not owned by the seller. You can also place limit and stop orders on ETF's. You can write covered options, which could enhance income returns. The first ETF (Spiders, with the ticker symbol SPY) is over ten years old and tracks the S&P 500. In addition to Spiders, popular ETF index funds include Diamonds/Dow Jones Industrial Average (symbol DIA) and Qubes (QQQ symbol), which tracks the NASDAQ 100. With ETFs you can diversify into almost every sector with minimal investment dollars (actually you could buy one share); some energy sectors share funds like the S&P Global Energy (ticker IXC), Dow Jones US Energy IYE, and Gold (GLD). The next level ETFs are being utilized by multi-sector money managers (not all as it is a passive investment and some managers argue they were not hired for a passive role). It should be interesting to see how they perform with higher management fees. Go to www.morningstar.com/cover/etf.html or www.sec.gov/answers/indexf.htmfor more information on index and ETF funds. Some investment companies now offer "baskets" of ETF funds.

- *Mutual funds* have been around for over eighty years and allow diversification and ownership of a wide variety of stocks or bonds with small amounts of investment capital. In addition, you get professional money management. The downside is that cost, fees, and commissions can be very high; the higher the turnover (buying and selling), the higher the potential capital gains and commission costs. You need to watch turnover in managers as well. Look at top holdings for any overlap, and watch the cost of fees, commissions, 12b-1 fees, and distribution costs. A good place to start is to check out www.personalfund.com (a paid subscription plan), which offers total cost of ownership and other fund comparisons. Most 401K plans utilize mutual funds, although as mentioned above, ETF's are being offered and becoming very popular in retirement plans. There is also no tax control; you pay capital gains tax every year on the capital gain distribution of the fund, and you receive a step-up in basis because of the tax paid, in nonqualified money. The fund can make money, pass on the capital gains tax to you, and you still could have lost money (not such a good deal). Most individuals repurchase more shares with the gains distributed at the end of the year (both qualified and nonqualified). If the fund's NAV is $10 and it pays a $5 capital gain, your new NAV would be $5; you hope the fund grows in value with the purchase of the additional shares. The fund distributes your tax on a 1099. You can deduct capital losses against capital gains (in nonqualified money) and up to $3,000 to offset ordinary income in any year. Any gain held less than one year is a short-term gain and is taxed at the individual's income tax rate. Any investment sold longer than one year is taxed at the current capital gain rate of 20% for tax payers in the 39.6% tax bracket and 15% for those in the 25-35% tax bracket and 0% for those in the 10-15% income tax bracket. **Tax Topic 409 - Capital Gains and Losses** http://www.irs.gov/taxtopics/tc409.html

- **Closed end funds** A closed-end fund may issue stocks or bonds and trades on an exchange or purchased from a broker. You buy or sell and receive market price at the time of the sale. Income and liquidity are generally the reasons people buy closed end funds. They use a higher leverage in the fix income portfolios (more risk) but better returns (higher the risk the better the returns). Such examples of closed end funds are PHK (PIMCO), FHY (First Trust). In addition, most closed end funds deliver a monthly income stream. Some companies are now offering a "basket" of closed end funds.

# Calculate Returns

To calculate your return on invested capital, price to earnings, and return on a mutual fund, use the following formula:

Current return on invested capital
Annual dividend                    $\underline{2.20}$ = 5% return
Current stock price                44.375

Price to earnings (P/E)
Current stock price                $\underline{44.375}$ = 10 times
EPS (earnings per share)           4.43  earnings

Return on mutual fund
$1 annual dividend

_____

$10 current offering price = 10% return

To see how you are really doing in comparison with the mutual fund published performance numbers, do the following:

1. Subtract your account balance at the start of the year from your current balance, divide the balance in half (including if it is negative), add back the money you had in the fund in the beginning of the year, and you have your average monthly balance.
2. From your current account balance, subtract both the amount you had in the fund at the start of the year and the additional investments. This gives you your total gain.
3. Divide your total gain or loss by your average monthly balance and multiply by 100. This gives you your dollar weighted total return for the year before taxes.

**Notes:**

_____

_____

_____

_____

_____

# Annuities: Protecting your Income and Beneficiaries

## Your will supersedes any 401K or IRA designations

> **TIP**: Almost 50% of all marriages end in divorce, be aware of splitting assets, if you have annuities or IRA's look at utilizing the 1035 tax-free transfer. If you transfer without using a 1035 you have (if under 59 ½) 10% tax penalty plus ordinary income. In addition with annuities you may have declining sales charges (CDSC) which can be as high as 8% of the total-you need to check with your annuity company for actual charges that you would incur or benefits you would each keep in the transfer to another annuity.

- *Annuities* are contracts issued by an insurance company that guarantee the investor will not run out of money through equal payments. Annuities also bypass the probate process, as they are beneficiary-designated products like life insurance, IRAs, etc. Most companies now offer living benefits (a guaranteed percentage, usually around 5% of the transfer value for the rest of your life regardless of the portfolio balance), annual ratchets (or the highest achieved portfolio balance) for death benefits minus any distributions, multiple investment choices, and spousal survivorship rights. This is where on death of the primary annuitant (owner of the contract); the surviving spouse assumes the contract and continues with income payments versus a lump sum distribution. The cost of annuities varies by the goodies you wish to attach to your contract such as estate riders, lifetime income, survivorship, and so on. You need to analyze these costs versus the benefit to you and your family. In essence, an annuity is buying insurance to protect your investment and future income. The annuity can run on an average an additional one percent for the insurance (and can vary by product) above mutual fund expenses—in most cases, it's not a bad deal.

*Some annuity options to consider:*

- By transferring lump-sum distributions from your 401(k), IRA, or pension plans into an annuity, you have now protected your investment with the guaranteed death benefit, which is the dollar amount you transferred into the annuity. you still have investment choices for future growth, which can give you a raise if your investments go up since the distribution is generally based on a percentage of the total portfolio.

- Pension plans generally give you three choices: 100 percent to you with no survivorship income to your spouse after you die, which is higher income payout; joint, which gives you less money monthly; or lump sum. You work thirty years, and they give you back a fixed amount for as long as you live. Your spouse will receive zero, if the single lifetime

Frank J. Eberhart, CEP®, RFC®

income option is chosen, or approximately 40 or 25 percent of that amount on your death if you chose the survivorship option. If you transferred that to an annuity, you would have a guaranteed death benefit, lifetime income stream, and the possibility for a raise because the income is based on a percentage of the total portfolio amount, and spousal options such as lump sum or continued income stream.

There is an age-old argument about whether mutual funds should be inside an IRA versus inside an annuity. For example, if you had $1 million in mutual funds in an IRA and $1 million in mutual funds inside an annuity and the day you died, the market crashed and they were both valued at $400,000, the mutual funds would pay $400,000 and the annuity would pay at least $1 million, less any distributions. You make the call. In addition, some companies offer an income rider that would provide income and death benefit at the highest water mark Vs. the income from the lower trashed balance

- With annuities, unlike life insurance, you do not need to take a physical exam to put money in them and to allow contributions or transfers up to age eighty-five or higher. Most companies require authorization for policies of $1 million or more.

- You have qualified and nonqualified annuities. Most people maximize their 401(k) or IRA, and then add to nonqualified annuities for additional tax-deferred investment growth.

- Current annuity owners with older policies may be better off completing a tax-free 1035 exchange for better products. Be careful that your death benefit is not higher than the portfolio value; once you transfer to a new policy, the dollar amount you transfer is your new dollar amount death benefit. Some companies offer bonus products to offset this. Again, be careful. The CDSC charges can be up to 8 percent or more and extend over ten years.

- All annuities (qualified or non-qualified) carry the 10 percent penalty if you take out distribution prior to age 59½. If you are under 59½, you can take distributions under IRS rule 72t. This allows equal periodic payments for a minimum of five years or an attained age of 59½ (without incurring the 10 percent penalty, you pay ordinary income tax)— whichever comes first.

- Equity-Index annuities: beware if you are looking for immediate income-it could be ten years or longer before you can actually receive any income. Furthermore, if you take prior distributions, you will probably incur huge penalties. The incentive for agents to sell this type of product is very high commissions. There are much better choices for income: buy bonds (treasury's or other high quality bonds), a variable or fixed annuity, high dividend paying stocks, closed end funds, and/or a combination of investments to help you achieve your income goals.

- Immediate annuities offer immediate payouts of a fixed income amount based on the portfolio size for the rest of your life.

- Variable annuities are generally used when deferred income is needed. The payouts fluctuate by the portfolio size and can offer more income if the underlying funds perform well. Usually variable annuities carry higher costs. You can have split buckets in a variable annuity-part of the money goes to a guaranteed fixed account and part goes to the variable side. What it accomplishes is over a certain period of time the money you put in is the worst you will do.

- **401K plans and annuities**. A popular approach is to transfer a certain dollar amount of your qualified plan into a variable annuity (this is generally only allowed for fewer than 50 employees); this gives the annuitant (you) a guaranteed death benefit and a guaranteed income stream for life. Remember that the qualified plan still owns the annuity, upon your death the annuity comes back into the plan and is then distributed to the beneficiaries, so it is important to take the compounding death benefit and income rider. If you retire, you can transfer the balance into the now IRA and you have lifetime income and spousal options.

Annuities require research. Don't be fooled with bells and whistles that have no value to you or your family. Ask what each extra feature costs, what the charges are for early liquidation and how long the charges apply, and what the features do for you.

Look at the financial strength of the insurance/annuity company. Go to www.sec.gov/answers/annuity.htm for more information.

## Bonds

Rich people don't buy bonds to get rich-they buy bonds to stay rich. A few basics for bonds; buying bonds should be for a long term or until maturity. If you paid par for the bond ($1,000 or face value) and the interest was 6%, you collect the interest until the maturity date and then you get back you $1,000 par value of the bond when they call it in for redemption.

If you buy at $900 and if the government agency, municipality, or company calls the bond, it is generally called "at par." This means you get the income from the coupon plus the capital gain from the cost less the sale price of $1,000 minus $900 cost = $100 gain, which also increases your yield. The lower the price of the bond, the higher the yield. Always check the yield to maturity and the yield to call on a bond. The coupon is your interest you collect from the par value (1,000 x 6 percent coupon is 60 per bond). The yield is what you make at maturity or early redemption that is your real return.

TIP: The next item for attention is doing a bid/ask into the secondary market before you buy. This does 2 things: one, it lets you know if there is a secondary resale market, and two, it tells what your bond is generally worth if you sell before maturity.

**All bonds have similar characteristics.** They represent the indebtedness, or liability, of their issuers in return for a specified sum, or principal. All debt has a maturity date, which is from one day to thirty years. Short-term debt is generally under one year to maturity, intermediate debt is one to ten years, and long-term debt is generally ten years or more. The bondholders receive a fixed interest rate usually for the lifetime of the bond duration. This is called the coupon rate. The rate of return for the interest is calculated two ways: current yield, which is the annual flow of interest or income, or yield to maturity, if the bond is held to maturity and redeemed at par value. Each debt agreement has obligations that must be met (stated in the legal documents), including the date of maturity, coupon rate, pledges of collateral, and any other conditions that must be met.

**There are two types of bonds.** *Bearer bonds* are coupon bonds that anybody can cash, since there are no names on the bonds to identify ownership. *Registered bonds* are issued in certificate form in the owner's name and are held in street name if in a brokerage account. All bonds carry ratings established by Moody's and Standard & Poor's. The ratings reflect the risk of owning the bonds: Moody's ratings are Aa3. A1, A2, Ba2; Standard & Poor's ratings are AA+, A, BBB+. Non-rated bonds are typically small municipalities or projects that cannot afford the cost of obtaining a rating from one of the rating agencies. Bonds carry risk of default, price fluctuations (if interest rates rise, bond prices fall; if interest rates fall, bond prices rise), and risk of inflation (not keeping up with inflation versus interest received). Most bonds have a *call* feature that allows their redemption prior to maturity. When you buy bonds, buy for yield, which is your true return. You need to look at yield to maturity and yield to call. The coupon or interest rate is based on par or $1,000, so if your coupon is 6 percent, your interest received would be $60 per bond, generally paid every six months. Bonds trade with interest to the settlement date unless otherwise stated. Corporate, municipal, and agency bond interest is based on a 30-day month and a 360-day calendar year.

Buying a bond-the interest or coupon from the bond is paid at par ($1,000) regardless what the value of the bond goes to (unless of course the bond defaults)

Calculating bond yields:

Annual interest $70

$$\frac{\text{Annual interest } \$70}{\text{Current market price } \$1{,}000} = \text{Current yield 7\%}$$

Calculating taxable yields:

Taxable equivalent = Tax-exempt yield

$$\frac{\text{Tax-exempt yield}}{\text{Yield}} \text{ 100\% tax bracket}$$

In other words, if you're tax-exempt yield is 4 percent and your tax bracket is 31 percent

4% Tax-exempt Yield = 4

$$\frac{4}{100\%-31\%} \quad \frac{4}{69\%} = .0579 \ (5.58)$$

**Calculating Bond Quote Pricing** Quotes are expressed as a percentage of face value or par amounts of $1,000. They are quoted in increments of eighths of $10: 1/8 of $10 = 1.25 or $1.25. So a quote of 90-1/8 of par would be $901.25. As mentioned previously, when buying bonds, you should look at the resale market, or secondary market, before you buy. You can have your financial adviser put in a bid-ask on the bond, which will provide you with the cost basis and whether there is a secondary market for resale

Notes:

_____

_____

_____

_____

_____

*Managed options and option writing* are what I refer to as "the other income." Very few people understand option trading. The Options Clearing Corporation (OCC) issues all options that are listed on the Chicago Board of Options Exchange (CBOE). If you're buying or selling, the standard option contract is for 100 shares or one option contract. All options expire at 3:30 PM Central Standard Time on the third Friday of the expiry month. All options (short-term profit or loss) are reported on Schedule D. You can offset short-term losses against long-term gains. In very general terms, if you own a stock and want to sell an option, you, as the owner of the stock, write or sell a "call option" if you think the stock is going to go up in value, or you sell a "put option" if you think the stock will decline. Owning the stock is considered covered-call writing; if the stock is called away, you get the premium for the call or put plus the difference of the strike price, which is the agreed price to buy or sell the security at a predetermined date.

Here is an example of an investor buying a put option (you think the stock is going lower, and you do not want to own the stock):

> Joe Investor buys a put option (he thinks the stock is going to go lower) on XYZ Company for a premium of $300. The underlying stock is at $40, which is the agreed strike price. If the stock drops to $30 per share on the open market, and the investor exercises the option and buys the stock at $30 and sells back to the writer of the put for $40, the profit would be $1,000 minus the $300 premium, or a net of $700. If the stock increases or stays the same, the investor would lose the $300 premium paid and the writer (owner of the stock) would keep the $300 premium.

This example is for buying a call option because you think the stock is going up and you do not want to own the stock:

> Joe Investor buys a call option on XYZ Company for $400 to buy 100 shares at $50 per share. The price goes to $70 during the option contract, the investor exercises the option to buy the stock at the agreed strike price of $50 per share and sells the stock on the open market for $70 per share; making $2,000 profit minus the $400 premium paid. If the stock does not increase or stays the same, the loss risk is limited to the $400 premium paid.

People buy or sell calls and puts to create income. You can do both, buy a put and call option on the same stock. It's like buying insurance; it lowers your overall profit because you can't win on both ends. The more "in the money" you are, the more likely the stock will get called away. "In the money" is if you sell a call at $1.50 per contract (one option contract is 100 shares of stock) for example, and the strike price is $25. Let's say the stock goes to $25.50 or above. The investor or buyer of the option will probably call the stock away and sell it at a later date on the open market to make money. You keep the premium and the difference to the strike price of the stock. If the stock price drops, the call will expire worthless, and you keep the premium and the stock. If you were the owner or writer of the stock, you hope nothing happens and you keep the stock and the premium paid. You wrote the options to increase your income and diversify your portfolio. If you are the buyer of the call or put, you are hoping you can buy the stock at the agreed prices and sell to make a profit. Short selling is a little more dangerous, because you are borrowing the stock from the broker and promising to repay with the same stock at a future date. There are many types of options, puts, calls, straddles, leaps, index options, covered calls, covered puts, naked options, and combinations. I find that when you utilize companies that specialize in options trading through individual funds or managed portfolios, you fare better than trying to guess the market as an individual. A great way to practice is to go to www.bigcharts.com and look under the Options tab, or go directly to the https://usequities.nyx.com/markets/nyse-mkt-equities (Formerly the American Stock Exchange www.amex.com). Covered-call writing is extremely useful for individuals who have a highly concentrated stock position with a low cost basis-you have a lot of stock you bought cheap and do not want to sell for capital gains and dividends, or it is restricted stock under rule 144. Companies will put your stock in a portfolio and write calls/puts, generate additional income, and protect the stock with the use of a margin account (borrowed money). This is used to protect the stock with cash to pay for the call versus selling the stock.

> Using options, you need to separate portfolio performance with income performance; otherwise, put your money in a total return investment. The portfolio may go up or down like any other stock portfolio, but you bought it for income, the option income is based on the number of shares you own or individual stocks with call writing options, cash flow is generated from premiums, capital gains, and dividends paid not the portfolio value.

For example, if you had $100,000 in a stock portfolio and $100,000 in an option portfolio (it is still a stock portfolio), they would both go up and down. The regular portfolio would yield around 1.1 percent, which is the average dividend yield, while the option portfolio would yield around 5-6 percent or more, plus capital gains (short-term) any interest accumulated, and you still get the dividend yield. Plus you can offset long-term gains with short-term losses-you can specify to sell at a loss, which gives you more cash that you can reinvest in other options. To illustrate further, the income on the 1.1 percent yield is around $1,100 per year, and the income on the option contract can be $6,000 or more per year. Option funds can generally generate more income because they have more dollars to spend on investments and receive additional inflows of cash. You can purchase equity traded option funds (closed-end) such as FFA, and others.

Notes:

_____

_____

_____

_____

_____

# Market, Limit, and Stop Orders

When you buy or sell a stock, it is referred to as T+3 (trade plus three days to settle). This means that you have that amount of time to pay money due or collect money from the sale.

When companies pay dividends, generally on a quarterly basis, you can take the cash or reinvest the dividend into the company stock. When you reinvest the dividends into the stock, you raise your cost basis and generally end up with odd lot or fractional shares of stock, which are difficult to sell. The board sets the record date on which you are entitled to receive the dividend; however, you must be a stockholder of record prior to that record date. The ex-dividend date (to be eligible for the dividend) is generally two business days before the record date. You buy auto insurance, homeowner's insurance, and life insurance to protect your homes, cars, and liabilities. So why not buy profit-and-loss protection with the use of limit orders, stop-loss orders, and so on? Here is how they work.

## Market Orders

- A *market order* is an order to buy or sell a stock immediately at the best execution price.

## Limit Orders

- A *limit order* is an order to buy or sell a security at a specified price or better for a specified time.
- A *buy limit* is the maximum price a buyer is willing to pay. If you want to buy a stock for $50 per share and the current price is $55 per share, you should put in a 50GTC (good 'til cancelled) order. The stock will be executed if it hits $50 or below.
- A *sell limit* is the minimum price a seller is willing to take for his or her security. If you bought a stock for $40 and the minimum amount you will take is $65, you would enter a sell limit order of 65GTC. The stock will not sell unless it hits at least $65 per share.

## Stop Orders

- *Buy stop orders* take advantage of increasing stock prices. If you bought the stock at $25 per share and think it will go to $35 per share, you would place a buy stop order at $35. If it hits $35, the order becomes a market buy order, the trade will be executed at the next trade price, and you will lock in your profit. If it never hits the target price, it will expire.
- *Sell stop orders* are used to stop a stock price from declining too low. Let's say you put in a sell stop at $50 and the current price is $65. If the price goes below $50, it will trigger the

sell order and convert it to a market order. The stock will sell at next price available, and you limit your losses.

- *Stop limit orders* help protect profit. If you bought a stock at $60 and it's currently at $75, which gives you a paper profit of $15 per share (it isn't a profit until you sell and put the money in your pocket), you put in a stop limit order. If the stock starts to decline and hits the stop price, it activates the trade. The sell stop limit says that if you put in $70 for the stop limit, you will get the next trade at $70 or above.

When the stockbroker pulls up his or her screen for equity trading and the broker places an execution order, the computer asks if it is a market order (immediate trade at market price), limit order, stop order, or stop and limit order. The price gets recorded and execution will take place at one end or the other, taking profit or protecting losses.

## Other types of risks to consider when deciding to purchase a security are as follows:

- Credit: the borrower's inability to repay the loan or debt
- Interest rate: the value of the bond will decline due to rising interest rates
- Inflation: the value of the asset will decline and will not keep up with inflation (bond interest); thus, your buying power is decreased
- Liquidity: the ability to sell the security
- Political climate: influences of government policies (both domestic and foreign) that affect values

  - *Selling short* is selling a security you do not own. Instead, you are borrowing from the broker, who in turn borrows from inventory, other margin customers, or other institutions that lend securities. You sell, or borrow, at the current market price and hope that the stock falls in price. You then buy the stock at the lower price, replace the borrowed stock to the broker, and profit from the difference. All short selling must be from a margin account. For example, if the shares sold short at $80 and the market drops to $60, the profit is $20 per share. The same could happen on the loss end of the deal: a stock bought at $80 goes to $100, leaving you with a loss of $20 per share.

  - *Selling short against the box* is when the investor actually owns the stock and wants to sell but not deliver the shares yet. He or she may pledge or use the stock to secure a loan and then later deliver the long shares to pay back the broker. This also defers any tax consequences of the sale.

- *Program trading*, which is becoming a large part of the volatility of Wall Street, is when institutional investors use computerized programs to trigger buy or sell orders. This can create large blocks of stocks in the market. If nobody buys, the price keeps dropping until it hits the desired target price of another investor. The same old rule applies: for every buyer there must be a seller, and for every seller there must be a buyer.

- The *OTC (over-the-counter) marketplace* is a negotiated marketplace between broker-dealers. The orders do not go through an exchange, but instead are completed via the telephone. Each broker-dealer firm has its own traders to handle the transactions. Most broker-dealers will not allow stop or limit orders on OTC securities because there is no specialist to handle or watch the price.[10] The pink sheets quote trades in the OTC market not traded on the NASDAQ. The NASDAQ trades more active OTC stocks. Other sources are newspapers.

- The *Instinet market* is when institutions trade between one another. Mutual fund companies, pensions, banks, and insurance companies provide one another with quotes on securities that they want to buy or sell.

- **Real estate investment trusts (REITs)** basically fall into two types: equity traded and direct ownership (closed end). All REITs pay out 90 percent of the revenues generated to the investors. Some provide a pass-through for depreciation for tax purposes. Real estate has recently been classified as the fourth asset class and is an asset that's noncorrelated to the stock market. Always check the types of properties inside a REIT. Higher-risk types include shopping malls, strip malls, apartment complexes, etc.; lower-risk types are class A office space with long-term leases and major corporations leasing the properties. Check the lengths and terms of the leases, holding periods for breakeven or redemption; how much leverage they have, meaning how much they borrow to buy the real estate; and whether they are triple-net leases, in which the lessee pays everything. Corporations pay rent from the operating budget, which means that they pay the rent before they pay stockholders or bondholders.

- **Direct-ownership REITs** (closed-end funds) give, in a sense, direct ownership of the real estate purchased inside the fund and pass through a portion of the real estate depreciation to the investor. Most offer a fixed rate of return and potentially increase

---

[10] Specialists hold a seat on the exchange and agree to maintain an orderly market in securities. They buy when others are selling, and they sell when others are buying. They buy and sell in their own account and act as agent for others. They must qualify with the board of exchange and have enough capital to maintain large positions in each security in which they specialize. Specialists handle most of the orders, from various brokers on the trading floor that cannot be executed immediately by the broker—stop orders, limit orders, and so on.

the yield over time. Average yield is from 6–8 percent annualized and compounded quarterly They are not as liquid, as they generally invest entirely in real estate and offer limited redemption; redemption at death or disability as per social security is usually 100 percent-anything less has a percentage around 10 percent from the NAV. If the REIT is paying 6 percent, the breakeven point would be around fourteen months. Most REITs have a one-year hold. The NAV[11] is usually fixed unless the funds offer a dividend reinvestment plan, at which time you buy more shares for less than the NAV. Closed-end REITs have a life expectancy at which time the investor must vote on what he or she wants to do: keep the income going by extending the fund, liquidate and take cash, or make it a publicly traded equity index fund, all of which is stated in the prospectus. You always need to check on the type of real estate for risk. Shopping malls, hotels, strip malls, and rental properties all generally carry higher risk than class A commercial properties.

---

**TIP:** If you want more liquidity and diversification from a closed-end REIT, take the cash dividend and buy equity traded REIT; you can now have additional growth and or sell off smaller quantities of shares. Understand closed-end REITs before you buy them.

---

- *Equity-traded REITs* trade like stocks on the open market. They are more volatile and invest in multiple strategies of real estate, hotels, other REITs, and preferred stocks. Visit www.nareit.com for more information.

- *Index funds* follow a particular index like the S&P 500, bond index, Russell 2000, etc. They are passive in nature, meaning that whatever stocks the fund owns, so do you. Index funds are for long-term investors who want to watch their investments grow. Index funds started in 1975, which gives you the opportunity to evaluate their track records. Index fund fees are generally lower than mutual fund fees, because managers only need to track a relatively fixed index of securities. Thus, there is less trading, which gives you a more favorable income tax position, lower realized capital gains tax, lower fees and expenses, and more work by computerization. Over the last twenty years, index funds have outperformed mutual funds by around 2.4 percent. The average expense ratio for mutual funds was around 1.3 percent, while index funds averaged around 0.2 percent. The differences include the fees that are incurred in mutual funds with sales loads and redemption fees, commissions from turnover of stock, and bond sales.

- *Managed commodity funds (mutual funds)* invest in raw materials such as wheat, corn, aluminum, copper, gas, and oil. These can be hedges against inflation; commodity prices

---

[11] Net asset value

tend to go up with inflation, while stock prices do better in declining inflation. Mutual funds are not allowed to buy commodities; they buy a derivative instrument, which is a contract whose value is based on the performance of an underlying investment, like a futures contract. These are noncorrelated assets to the market. Managed commodities funds can potentially help reduce risk and enhance overall performance.

- *1031 real estate transfers* offer tax solutions for real estate investors (if you actually own the real estate) to defer capital gains tax. The IRS code allows a property owner to sell one real estate asset and buy another similar property without incurring (deferring) capital gains tax. Typically individuals with highly appreciated properties where they have a low cost basis and the current value is high from appreciation. An example would be vacant property where you sell non-income-producing land and reinvest into some form of commercial rental income-producing real estate. Always consult a tax adviser, as the rules can get quite complicated. In simple form, it works like this: You sell your property, and the proceeds go into escrow with a qualified intermediary (most 1031 exchange companies can find you an intermediary). Within forty-five days of the sale of your relinquished property, you must notify the qualified intermediary of the intent to replace your property with the 1031-identified property. The companies will provide lists of properties they have to offer for exchange. If, after forty-five days, you have not identified your replacement property, you pay tax on the sale. Once you identify the replacement property, you sign all the agreements and you start enjoying income from the new property as a landlord, without all the headaches and maintenance. The total process must be completed within a total of 180 days of the final sale of the relinquished property. Always check with your tax adviser and the 1031 exchange company for exit strategies if you wish to sell your share of the newly acquired property. For more information, call 1-800-IRS-1031, search for "1031 exchanges" on the Internet, and for a qualified intermediary.

- *Fund of funds* are mutual funds investing in a basket of other mutual funds. They have a management team overseeing, rebalancing, reallocating, and handling due diligence (making sure the funds meet and maintain the requirements, objectives, and performance) of the basket of funds in the portfolios. Some hedge funds use this strategy as well. The investment management company Horizon Investments uses a different strategy and asset reallocation called "dynamic asset allocation and rebalancing." This is an active strategy that varies the portfolio composition in response to changing market conditions and expectations. Asset classes with the most profit potential are given more weight than weaker asset classes. This is similar to static asset allocation in its use of diversification to reduce volatility, but it differs in its ability to reallocate funds to the current market leadership and away from market laggards.

> *TIP:* Make sure you understand the various layers of fees involved with fund of funds before you invest. Take the time to evaluate the fees versus performance, this goes for any investment-the more you understand the better your outcome.

- *Hedge funds* number around eight thousand; some are SEC[12]-registered and some are not. Hedge funds come under the Investment Company Act of 1940 and invest in various, generally non-correlated, securities to the market. Most managers have a vested interest in the portfolios, since they themselves have a great deal of money invested in their own hedge funds. They are paid on performance and use a targeted-return approach. Some of the strategies used include investing in currencies, short sales of securities, leveraged (borrowed) money, futures, and options on futures, index options, and arbitrages. Hedge funds generally are used to offset the markets, enhance performance, and reduce risk. Some are "fund of funds," which use the strategies of many managers who oversee the portfolios, allowing for many different strategies in one account. In recent years, the minimum dollar required investment amounts have been reduced to as low as $50,000 and $100,000 for accredited investors.[13] Compensation (manager's fees) and bonuses based on performance over the targeted (hurdle) return are fund costs. If the targeted return is 7 percent and the fund does 10 percent, the managers are paid anywhere from 10–20 percent of the money over the targeted hurdle, not on the entire portfolio. Many pensions and wealthy individuals have used hedge funds to have a non-correlated investment to the stock market. In some cases, managed portfolios have incorporated a "hedge fund to fund" and "commodity fund" inside the standard asset classes of large-cap value, growth, small/mid-cap, international, and bond ETFs or managed bond portfolios—all in one account.

- *Managed money* includes individual stocks and bonds. In the past, you hired a money manager for around $100,000 investment per manager per asset class or style (large-cap value, mid-cap, and the style might be moderate or aggressive). This was with the idea that he or she would diversify your portfolio and theoretically do a better job than you could because of access to resources. Several problems ensued. First, to diversify into five asset classes, you would need over $500,000 and at least another $500,000+ to invest in hedge funds. Second, each manager didn't know the other existed, so you had potential overlap, and wash sale rules were in effect, which could affect taxation. Third, there was no rebalancing. The money managers kept investing, thinking that this would last forever, which it didn't and that they could beat the benchmarks—meaning

---

[12] Securities and Exchange Commission

[13] Accredited investors are generally individuals with a net worth of $1-1.5 million.

Frank J. Eberhart, CEP®, RFC®

that if the S&P 500 was the unmanaged benchmark index and the S&P was down 20 percent and they were down 16 percent, they beat the benchmark. However, you still lost 16 percent while they were slapping hands over their victory and got paid quite nicely. Not so hot for you.

- *New-era managed portfolios* are how I describe a process that, in fairness, some mutual funds also use. Money managers have embraced the concept of combining five to seven asset classes in one account, instead of getting five or more separate and confusing statements for each account, with an overlay manager who makes sure that money managers are talking to each other. This helps eliminate overlap of securities and achieve better diversification. Many money managers also do a daily evaluation and rebalancing. The accounting world did not embrace this, but the IRS now allows the accountants to attach a broker statement[14] showing all trades and cost basis for profit and loss without the accountants to manually complete this tedious entry work. Additional advantages of direct money managers include control of the process; the ability to see what the managers are doing on a daily basis with around-the-clock online access, which helps you make decisions for any changes; the ability to make changes immediately to the portfolio; and control of costs meaning you know exactly what you are paying in fees, and the fees are generally tax deductible.    The disadvantage is that you see the fee on a quarterly basis, so you need to get over the impact of this large sum of money being withdrawn from the account. Your mutual funds and other investment vehicles may, and probably do, cost more.

What you *can't* see *can* hurt you. Fees directly affect performance. With the fixed costs, i.e. money manager that charges a flat fee, you can quickly determine whether the fee is worth the performance.

---

[14] The IRS requires you to record all profit-and-loss transactions on your tax return.

# Investment Checklist

- Does it meet your investment objectives, risk profile, and time frame?

- What are the risks with this fund or investment?

- What is the liquidity (how easy can you sell this investment and at what cost)?

- What is the overlap (same stocks or bonds held) of top holdings in each of the funds you pick?

- What is the investment objective of the fund or manager?

- Is the portfolio manager turnover high? How long have the current managers managed the fund?

- What is the portfolio turnover ratio? The higher the turnover (trading), the higher the cost, because you pay for commissions on trades inside the fund.

- Keep track of what you paid for the investment, not the advertised yields or stated returns. You can then see what you would get back if you sell it later. See step 8a.

- Pay attention to current returns—not just the one-, three-, five-, or ten-year returns, as they can be deceiving. You could put in $10,000 during a bad year or midyear and lose money, but the fund will show a positive return for each of the periods. *You need a blend of equity and bonds, cash, and alternative investments to stay ahead of the game.*

- Ask for current; three-month and one-, two-, and three-year performance numbers and after-tax return numbers. A good Web page for looking at fund performance and costs (it's unaudited) is www.sec.gov/cgi-bin/srch-edgar .

- Remember, past performance is no guarantee of future results or performance.

- If the fund is underperforming in comparison with other similar funds, then sell and move your money to a better fund. Check out the Web site www.personalfund.com and www.marketwatch.com for comparisons to other funds, expense ratios, yields, and returns as well as costs to own the fund and trading costs.

- Does the broker/bank, mutual fund company, or annuity company offer investment policies?[15]

- Consider cost of ownership, which includes redemption fees, turnover (how often the money managers trade stocks/bonds), commissions, taxes, 12b-1 fees, manager fees, and distribution fees (higher fees mean lower returns). Read the prospectus.

- Consider sales commissions (front-end loads are charges you pay up front, which reduce your investment by that amount). Don't confuse load/no-load with fund fees, commissions on trading costs, 12b-1 fees, and manager fees.

- Does the fund offer break points on purchases? Make sure you keep track. Don't let a broker put you into multiple funds to avoid giving you break points, as it affects his commission. You can also sign a letter of intent (LOI) that states your intention to make your investment total the break-point level over the next thirteen months. If you do not meet the break-point level, you may have to pay back the difference. You can also backdate a LOI for ninety calendar days.

- Class B shares are no-load and up front, but they have declining sales charges (CDSC) over a specified period of time—know what they are, how much, and how long. You also incur 12b-1 fees. After the CDSC charges are gone, they convert to class A shares.

- Consider annual charges, which are fees generally charged for smaller accounts and IRAs. Fees vary. Expense ratios are what the internal fund charges for managers and 12b-1 fees (the funds charged for advertisement). Pay attention to turnover in a mutual fund: the higher the turnover (buying and selling), the more it adds to the cost of ownership. You, the investor, pay commissions every time a trade is made, and the commission trades are not listed in the management or fund costs. You need to dig deep in the prospectus to find them. A great Web page that includes the total cost of ownership, including turnover costs, is www.personalfund.com. It has several options for pricing. If you invest mainly in mutual funds, it's worth the approximate $200 annual subscription. It also gives you comparable funds with lower costs. You can also visit www.sec.gov/cgi-bin/srch-edgar (Securities and Exchange Commission) for unaudited mutual fund, annuity, and company reports and other useful information.

- Ask for after-tax returns. Mutual fund companies now must report them.

---

[15] Investment policies provide protection for all. They specify your risk tolerance, type of investments, investment style (conservative, moderate, and so on), and objectives. The policy puts everything in writing and should be reviewed periodically as your life events change.

- First rule of thumb: take your highest point of growth and put a stop-loss or limit order (see step 8) in place to protect your profit or limit your loss. For example, if you have $100,000 and it grows to $115,000, from $115,000 you might place a stop order at a loss of 10 percent from the high, or-$11,500, which still leaves you a profit of $3,500. Each individual investor can establish his or her own percentage of comfort. You can do the same with individual money managers, and with individual stocks with limit and stop-loss orders, which are discussed later.

- Second rule of thumb: you need to take the emotion out of investing; it is about buying low and selling high and making a *profit*. Let's get real here. If you sell a stock, bond, mutual fund, or any other security, don't act like somebody cut off your arm! If you bought the stock at $25 per share and sold for $40 per share in the same year, and your tax bracket was 30 percent, you made $40-$25 = $15 per share profit. Multiply by 30 percent for your capital gains tax of $4.50 per share, and you have $10.50 per share net profit! That's a 70 percent profit and 85 percent profit if you hold it one year or longer!

- Ask the brokerage firm, bank, or Mutual Fund Company whether it offers investment policies. Investment policies are the terms and conditions of your investment risk tolerance and comfort level. They spell out whether you are a conservative or moderate investor and help protect you from anybody going outside your comfort zone. You need to understand more about the downsides of arbitration and mediation contracts that you sign with brokerage houses. Always keep track of your original purchase price and your original confirmation tickets from the brokerage or fund company when you buy or sell any security.

Understanding the previous checklist and information in this book can help you make the right selections in mutual funds, ETFs, managed money, bonds, REITs, hedge funds, commodities, options, and fee structures.

# How to Help Choose an Adviser

The first thing you need to do before selecting an adviser is to determine your goals. Using this workbook will help you understand your options, and direct potential brokers/bankers/accountants who wish to vie for your money. Have them explain how they get paid—by commission, fee only, advisory fees, or a combination. You want no surprises. Ask if they have an investment policy, what their education is, what licenses they hold, what designations they have, what their specialty is, and what their arbitration requirements are (if they have standard or triple arbitration, and so on). After you are comfortable with the answers, ask for a full proposal in writing for an estate plan, retirement plan, investment strategy, insurance quotes, and tax planning. Ask about any Web pages that have financial calculators for you to use. Here are some Web pages you can use to check out the adviser: www.finra.com for any complaints and securities records.

| | |
|---|---|
| www.finra.com | National Association of Securities Dealers |
| www.cfp.net | Certified Financial Planner Board of Standards |
| www.naic.org | National Association of Insurance Commissioners |
| www.sec.gov | Securities and Exchange Commission |
| www.advisorinfo.sec.gov | SEC investment adviser public disclosure |
| www.nicep.org | National Institute of Certified Estate Planners |
| www.iarfc.org | International Association of Registered Financial Consultants |

- *Certified financial planners (CFPs)* are individuals who have passed various tests and have conformed to the CFP board's code of ethics.

- *Certified estate planners (CEPs)* are individuals who have passed various tests and have complied with a code of ethics. They are required to maintain additional and ongoing certified estate courses.

- *Registered investment advisers (RIAs)* must complete ADV forms and register with the SEC for full disclosure and history of the company and the individual. RIA is not a designation and must be spelled out on any form of communication.

- *Chartered life underwriters (CLUs)* are insurance salespersons.

- *Chartered financial consultants (CHFCs)* are insurance agents entering into the financial marketplace.

- *Charted financial analysts (CFAs)* are generally securities analysts who work for larger institutions.

- *Certified public accountants (CPAs)* are tax specialists who are required to have a formal education and maintain ongoing certified estate education.

- *Registered financial consultants (RFCs)* require ongoing certified estate testing.

Do your homework, follow through, and check out your advisers to make sure they are legitimate and what they say they are: www.finra.com

# Book 4: Book of Business

Don't just be in business to stay in business-be in business to grow your business-*profitably*. From Mom & Pop shops to small and medium size (and large) businesses, you need more than just the essentials for maintaining your business and future growth, you need a complete plan. All the above information is needed for your personal planning; now let's discuss your business planning. Incorporating a solid budget, safeguarding your business and business assets, best practices, including marketing strategies, SEO (search engine optimization) development for web sites, seminars, workshops, and more. We will also discuss health care accounts in particular HSA programs, defined contribution plans, IRS Audits, Compliance dealing with ERISA, PCI compliance for credit cards, 401K, Payroll, FMLA, and Section 105 and 125 plans.

Most companies are out of compliance in areas such as: not filing 5500 for health care and 401(k) plans,not providing summary plan descriptions (ERISA) for health insurance to plan participants, not doing due diligence on their 401(k) or other qualified plans. Due diligence on these plans includes proper fund selections, monitoring fund performance, conducting quarterly meetings, adequate disclosure of fees and costs to plan participants, not filing new section 125 plans if they change payroll companies (which means you are illegally deducting health premiums on a pre-tax basis), not following the 7 day rule for timely deposits from payroll to the employees retirement accounts for investing. You won't like the fines and penalties for non-compliance in any of these areas.

Most companies have not rewritten their defined contribution plan documents as required by IRS in 2010. What does all that mean? Big fines, big hassles, time, and money, potential participant law suits, etc.

We will discuss how to correct these issues. Let's start with a simple budget (next page).

- Your budget should be entered in spread sheet in excel or other format that can be updated and contain all 12 months.
- Make of Vehicles serial numbers
- Operators of the vehicle driver's license and expiration dates
- Credit card numbers and any employees who are assigned a card
- Cell phone numbers and serial numbers and employees who own that and any laptops/tablets
- **Add your own categories as needed (such as workman's comp, buy/sell or key man insurance)**
- List your current inventory and record end of year inventory
- Record all your policy numbers (categorized)
- Bank loans, or other loans all account numbers
- **ADD any category that fits your business profile**

**Many of these items can be accomplished automatically with Payroll (we do with our HR package)**

# Business Budget

**Make a copy for each month: put in a binder or excel spreadsheet**

Month_____     Beginning Cash Balance: $_____

| Category | Estimated Budget | Actual | Difference |
|---|---|---|---|
| Revenue/1099 | _____ | _____ | _____ |
| Accounts receivable | _____ | _____ | _____ |
| Investment Income | _____ | _____ | _____ |
| Interest Income | _____ | _____ | _____ |
| Other | _____ | _____ | _____ |
| **Total Income:** | $_____ | | |

EXPENSES:

| Category | Estimated Budget | Actual | Difference |
|---|---|---|---|
| Rent/Lease | _____ | _____ | _____ |
| Loans | _____ | _____ | _____ |
| Accounts Payable | _____ | _____ | _____ |
| Inventory Purchases | _____ | _____ | _____ |
| Equipment Purchases | _____ | _____ | _____ |
| Office Supplies | _____ | _____ | _____ |
| Cell Phones | _____ | _____ | _____ |
| Phone/Fax/Internet | _____ | _____ | _____ |
| Advertising | _____ | _____ | _____ |
| Printing | _____ | _____ | _____ |
| USPS | _____ | _____ | _____ |
| UPS/FedEx | _____ | _____ | _____ |
| Payroll | _____ | _____ | _____ |
| Payroll Taxes/fees | _____ | _____ | _____ |
| Health Insurance | _____ | _____ | _____ |
| Repairs/Maintenance | _____ | _____ | _____ |
| Vehicle Payments | _____ | _____ | _____ |
| Vehicle Insurance | _____ | _____ | _____ |
| Vehicle Maintenance | _____ | _____ | _____ |
| Business Insurance | _____ | _____ | _____ |
| Life/disability Insurance | _____ | _____ | _____ |
| Accounting/legal fees | _____ | _____ | _____ |
| Technology Purchases | _____ | _____ | _____ |

Frank J. Eberhart, CEP®, RFC®

| | | | |
|---|---|---|---|
| Retirement Contributions | _____ | _____ | _____ |
| Subscription/dues | _____ | _____ | _____ |
| Web hosting fees | _____ | _____ | _____ |
| Other | _____ | _____ | _____ |

*Total Expenses:*   $_____

*Total Income:* _____ *(minus)* *Total Expenses:* _____ = *Ending Balance:*_____

No matter how big or small your business is: Regardless of how you accept payments, internet, card swipe, wireless, Moto, desktop, recurring, plug n pay …You need to Validate Your PCI Compliance

# Best Practices

## VALIDATE Your PC

Cyber criminals are taking aim at smaller merchants who are less likely to be compliant with PCI standards, according to a recent Verizon Business report by Jen Mack, a former member of the PCI Security Standards Council. The report found that the most common attack methods are malware and hacking, SQL injections, and exploitation of default or guessable credentials. Most data breaches happen because merchants fail to make sure that security mechanisms are properly deployed. Mack says Level 3 and Level 4 retailers are being targeted by cyber thieves looking to steal...

* Beginning January 1, 2011 merchants are to validate the latest PCI DSS document labeled Version 2.0. That will include the New Self-Assessment Questionnaire; the Attestation of Compliance still remains Version 2.0.

## Many Things That Can Help Prevent Security Breaches Are Simple to Implement and May Be Required by the Payment Card Industry Data Securty Standard (PCI DSS):

- Buy and use only PA-DSS validated terminals and payment software at your point of sale, or installed website shopping cart for e-commerce.
- For payment related services like gateways, e-commerce solutions or external billing management, make sure the vendors are compliant with PCI DSS.
- Do not store any cardholder data in computers or on paper.
- Use a firewall on your network and PCS and separate your payment environment from the internet or wireless usage.
- Use strong system passwords (Never use default password supplied by vendors).
- Assign unique system user ID's per employee and enable/track access logs.
- Visually inspect your POS equipment and card readers for signs of tampering.
- Teach your employees about security and protecting cardholder data.
- Comply with the PCI DSS standard: HTTPS://WWW.PCISECURITYSTANDARD.ORG/MERCHANTS/

## Cardholder Data Can Be Stolen from Many Places, Including:

- Paper receipts and imprints stored insecurely (applies to dial out terminals and touch tone merchants).
- Data stored electronically in a payment system database.
- Compromised card readers.
- Unsecured wireless networks on premises.

Frank J. Eberhart, CEP®, RFC®

## Who needs to comply with the PCI DSS?

All organizations, regardless of size or number of transactions, that process, store or transmit cardholder data must comply with the PCI DSS. Essentially, all merchants with a Merchant Identification number (MID) and all service providers that touch cardholder data are required to comply with the PCI DSS.

## What happens if I do not comply?

Merchants that do not comply with PCI DSS may be subject to fines, card replacement costs, costly forensic audits, brand damage, etc., should a breach event occur. Many acquiring banks are issuing fines for merchants who do not comply with PCI. For a little upfront effort and cost to comply with PCI, you greatly help reduce your risk from facing these extremely unpleasant and costly consequences.

## My shopping cart/payment gateway/processing is outsourced, why is this my responsibility? If I am breached, wouldn't it be their fault?

Merely using a third-party company does not exclude a company from PCI compliance. It may cut down on your risk exposure and consequently reduce the effort to validate compliance. However, it does not mean you are exempt from PCI. All merchants are required to complete the SAQ annually at a minimum. It also addresses internal security practices and procedures behind handling credit card data. One of the leading causes of data breaches is due to employee error or carelessness when handling sensitive information- this is why proper policies should be in place and a formal Security Awareness Training should be conducted. Your business must protect cardholder data when you receive it, and process charge backs and refunds. You must also ensure that providers' applications and card payment terminals comply with respective PCI standards and do not store sensitive cardholder data. You should request a certificate of compliance annually from providers.

## My payment application is already compliant- what else do I need to do?

Utilizing a compliant payment application is a best practice towards achieving compliance, but PCI compliance also covers data security, physical security and network security.

A **network security scan** involves an automated tool that checks a merchant or service provider's systems for vulnerabilities. The tool will conduct a non-intrusive scan to remotely review networks and Web applications based on the external-facing Internet protocol (IP) addresses provided by the merchant or service provider. The scan will identify vulnerabilities in operating systems, services, and devices that could be used by hackers to target the company's private network. As provided by an Approved Scanning

Vendors (ASV's) the tool will not require the merchant or service provider to install any software on their systems, and no denial-of-service attacks will be performed. **Note:** typically only merchants with external facing IP address are required to have passing quarterly scans to validate PCI compliance.

## Do I need vulnerability scanning to validate compliance?

If you electronically store cardholder data post authorization, or if your processing systems have any internet connectivity, a quarterly scan by a PCI SSC Approved Scanning Vendor (ASV) is required.

## How often do I have to scan?

Every 90 days/once per quarter you are required to submit a passing scan.

## I do not want this service:

Due to the importance of securing cardholder information and the requirements mandated by the Payment Card Industry Data Security Council we are unable to waive this fee but will continue to work hard at offering you the best compliance services as inexpensively as possible. All merchants that accept credit cards, regardless of size or sales volume, must validate PCI compliance at least annually. There is no way around this. Although larger merchants are at a greater risk of a security breach due to their processing volumes, statistics show that small (Level 4) merchants account for over 85% of compromise events.

## Can I switch to a new processor who doesn't require compliance?

All Acquirers are responsible for ensuring that all of their merchants comply with the PCI Data Security Standard (DSS) requirements, therefore, all processors are required by the card brands to implement a PCI compliance program. We have partnered with Panoptic Security based on the fact that they provide the best value for our merchants and provide full support in helping you in the compliance process.

## What is the cost associated with a compliance failure or data breach?

The cost associated with a compliance failure or data breach can be very expensive for any merchant, especially a small or medium sized business owner. These costs include:

- Forensic investigation of computer or point of sale systems: $10,000-$20,000
- Reimbursement for fraudulent purchases made using breached information, as well as chargeback fees for those transactions

- Replacement cards for breach accounts: $3-$10 per card
- Card Association fines for non-compliance with the PCI Standard, up to $500,000
- Loss of business reputation and customer loyalty, and potentially credit card acceptance
- Potential listing in the MATCH

## **As a merchant, aren't I entitled to store any data?

Many merchants believe that they own the customer and have a right to store all the data about that customer in order to help their business. Not only is this incorrect regarding PCI, it may also be a violation of State and Federal legislation regarding privacy. The PCI regulations specifically forbid storing of any of the following:

- Unencrypted credit card number
- CVV or CVV2
- Pin blocks
- PIN numbers
- Track 1 or 2 data

Any of the above found in databases, log files, audit trails, backups etc. at a merchant can result in serious consequences for the Merchant, especially if a compromise has taken place.

I can just answer 'yes' to all the criteria on the Self-Assessment Questionnaire (SAQ). NO

Source: www.infosecurityanalysis.com
Source: Verizon Business Data Breach Report*

**What to do if compromised:**
http://usa.visa.com/merchants/risk_management/cisp.html

- **Forensics audit** costs: $8,000 to $20,000
- **Card replacement costs:** generally between $3 and $10 per card
- **Brand damage:** Hard to quantify but at the end of the day, this could be the most damaging consequence to a business
- **Compliance fines:** Currently range from $5,000 to $250,000 depending on the size of the breach and the nature of the offense that led to the compromise

## Card Compromise Trends

Over the last couple of years it became imperative that all merchants who print, process, transmit or store credit card information must meet the requirements set forth by the Payment Card Industry Data Security Standard (PCI DSS). When you hear about security breaches it is most often about the large corporations such as Heartland, TJX and others, however over 85% of breaches that occur are of smaller companies. The common misconception is that smaller companies feel that they would not be impacted because of their size of business and/or volume of sales. However, a hacker does not look for the size of company or the estimated amount of sales. Their only interest is the vulnerabilities to retrieve sensitive credit card data.

Areas of major concern for breaches: Virus's, worms, stolen computers, 3rd party default, credit card theft, grocery chains, restaurants, etc. small to mid – size business are most effected by breaches.

## Defined Contribution, Pension, Profit Sharing, Deferred Comp, Executive Plans, Insurance

*Employer notice*:

As a company offering 401(k) and Profit Sharing Plans, I think it is important to understand ERISA[16] and Department of Labor (DOL) laws and how they affect you and your employees.

Erisa Section 402(b)(1) requires that every employee benefit plan provide a procedure for establishing a funding policy and method consistent with the objectives of the plan and the requirements of Erisa, Department of Labor (DOL) urges it to be in writing.

Further, the Department of Labor (DOL) requires all employee salary deferrals to be contributed to the Plan as soon as administratively feasible, regulations say the deferral should not to exceed 15 business days after the end of the month in which the salary deferral occurred. Keep in mind that DOL does not recognize the 15-day rule.

**IMPORTANT ALERT:** DOL during an audit will (they are really focusing on this) check your deposits, if they find a 3 day salary deferral deposit and all subsequent deposits were 10 days, they will charge you the performance difference for the plan throughout the life of the contract!

In simpler terms, an investment policy (we have provided guidelines to establishing an investment policy and the use of TPA'S-third party administrator later). An investment policy should be in writing and clearly state the objectives philosophy and goals of the plan, identify the standards and selection of appropriate investments, acceptable risk and return ratios, benchmarks for investment performance and proper monitoring of the investments. In 1992 DOL issued regulations under ERISA Section 404 (C) sets forth-specific rules that must be carried out in order for plan fiduciaries to afford themselves the relief from liability. As the employer you are the fiduciary of

---

[16] Employee Retirement Income Security Act of 1974, ERISA

the plan, and are potentially liable for up to the full value of your estate and subject the plan to lose its tax-free status.

ERISA also requires all fiduciary of employees trusts be covered by a surety bond equal to at least 10% of the trusts (401(k) assets, of which the minimum is $1,000 and the maximum is $500,000. This bond only covers fraud and theft; it does not cover the ERISA or DOL requirements or alleviate the trustee or fiduciaries liability from the plan.

Keep in mind of your due diligence, if you delegate fiduciary responsibility for management and control of plan assets to any person other than an investment manager as defined by ERISA you are liable for that person's actions.

To learn more on this go to www.erisa.com

## Helpful Web page links:

| | |
|---|---|
| www.erisa.com | Employee Retirement Income Securities Act |
| www.irs.gov/retirement-plans | IRS |
| www.dol.gov/ebsa | Department of Labor |
| www.pbgc.gov | Pension Benefit Guaranty Corporation |
| www.FINRA.com | National Association of Securities Dealers |
| www.401khelpcenter.com | Help with 401K questions |
| www.mhco.com | Mckay-Hochman up to date information on law or policy changes |
| feberhart.mybenefitadvisor.com | My benefit web site |
| www.preferredpension.com | TPA/Administrator |

# Retirement Plan Overview

As an employer, which defined contribution, plan is right for your business and employees?

There are many types of qualified retirement plans to fit your needs. They are important to have a plan to attract new and keep current employees to tax sheltering income, and tax deductions for the business.

Qualified plans must meet certain requirements established by the IRS, including minimum participation, vesting, and funding requirements. The IRS in return provides significant tax advantages to businesses and participants including:

- Employer contributions are tax-deductible
- Earnings on investments accumulate tax-deferred
- Employees are not taxed on contributions until they receive or withdraw the funds
- Employees make pre-tax contributions
- On-going plan expenses are tax deductible, check with your accountant

As an employer, you are fiduciary and trustee to these plans even if you have investment managers. Education, due diligence, plan and fund selection, reviews of funds, for you and your employees is essential and required. If you have a brokerage, annuity, bank, or Mutual Fund Company installed retirement plan, make sure they offer educational meetings, offer frequent reviews of performance, teach you and your employees how to access the web page, and how to understand what they are looking at. Most companies only offer 800 numbers and no advice; I find this a totally unacceptable practice. As fiduciary and trustee of these plans you need to have some safeguards in place to protect you and your employees. Ultimately, you are fiduciary and trustee. The new ERISA Section 3(38) Fiduciary Rule can help:

## ERISA Section 3(38) Fiduciary

Section 3(38) is an "investment manager" and by definition is a fiduciary because they take discretion, authority and control of the plan's assets. ERISA provides that a plan sponsor can delegate the significant responsibility (and significant liability) of selecting, monitoring and replacing of investments to the 3(38) investment manager fiduciary. A 3(38) fiduciary can only be (a) a bank, (b) an insurance company, or (c) a registered investment adviser (RIA) subject to the Investment Advisers Act of 1940 (such as GBS Investment Consulting, LLC). Once a 3(38) is properly named, the plan sponsor effectively hands over authority to the 3(38) fiduciary to make investment decisions. The 3(38) fiduciary therefore assumes legal responsibility and liability for the decisions it makes, which enables the plan sponsor to better manage and mitigate their fiduciary risk. However, a point that is often overlooked is that the plan sponsor cannot completely eliminate its fiduciary liability. The plan sponsor is still responsible for the prudent selection of the 3(38) investment manager and must monitor and benchmark that 3(38) investment manager. Also, if the plan sponsor overrides the decisions of the 3(38) advisor, the plan sponsor assumes the responsibility and liability.

## The following are guidelines that should be in place:

An investment policy should include:

- General investment philosophy and objectives of the plan for short, intermediate and long-term
- Specific standards for identifying and selecting investments for short, intermediate and long-term and composition of the portfolio with regards to diversification and projected returns and liquidity
- Risk and return profiles for each employee
- Benchmarks for investment performance
- Procedures for monitoring and evaluating the investments, funding methods, and the plan documents at least once per year
- Diversification and rebalancing strategies (making sure there is very little overlap of investment choices) with a diversified portfolio
- Outline the responsibilities of each party associated with the Plan including the Advisor, Custodian/Trustee, and any specific instructions for any money managers used or Investment Policies they provide
- Outlining responsibilities for procedures for controlling investment and Plan expenses, which should include; money managers fees and any trading costs, annual fees, trading costs, distribution costs, and 12b-1 fees for mutual funds, Advisor or consulting fees, custodial charges, and any administrative charges for services provided by an investment manager or TPA[17]
- ERISA requires all fiduciaries and trustees to buy a bond to cover employee losses against theft, it does not relieve the trustee/fiduciary from their responsibilities of investment prudence and due diligence.

Due diligence is a requirement on the employer to make sure all of the above items are in compliance. It protects you, the employees, the brokers, mutual fund companies, and keeps DOL, ERISA, and the IRS from implementing undo punishment.

---

[17] TPA third party administrator, it can be from a turnkey operation provided by a Mutual Fund Company, Insurance Company, or outside TPA that performs all aspects of the Plan including 5500 and testing.

# 401(K) Plan Checklist

|    |                                                                                                                              |     |    |
|----|------------------------------------------------------------------------------------------------------------------------------|-----|----|
| 1. | Has your plan been updated within the past few years? <br> New rules have been implemented including 3(38) and 408(b)(2)       | Yes | No |
| 2. | Are the plans operations based on the plan document?                                                                          | Yes | No |
| 3. | Do you have an Investment Policy Statement?                                                                                   | Yes | No |
| 4. | Were employers matching contributions made to all appropriate employees under the terms of the plan?                          | Yes | No |
| 5. | Has the plan satisfied the 401(k) nondiscrimination tests (ADP & ACP)? (This is annual testing)                               | Yes | No |
| 6. | Were all the eligible employees identified and given the opportunity to make elective deferral elections?                     | Yes | No |
| 7. | Are elective deferral limited to the amounts under IRC402(g) for the calendar year?                                           | Yes | No |
| 8. | Have you timely deposited employee elective deferrals? <br> Deposits are required as soon as they can be segregated from employer assets | Yes | No |
| 9. | Do participant loans conform to the requirements of the plan document and IRC 72(p)?                                          | Yes | No |
| 10. | Were hardship distributions made properly?                                                                                   | Yes | No |
| 11. | Have you filed your 5500?                                                                                                     | Yes | No |
| 12. | Have you filed your 5500 for your welfare benefits?                                                                           | Yes | No |
| 13. | Is the plans definition of compensation for all deferrals & allocations used correctly?                                      | Yes | No |

A common error according to Plan auditors if the incorrect definition of compensation is used (i.e. you include overtime income that was specifically excluded) all of the testing is wrong because it is using incorrect deferral percentages because the compensation is wrong. This checklist is only a guideline and not a complete list of plan requirements. You should always do an annual review of your plan with your TPA/Advisor. You should understand Fiduciary/trustee responsibilities and how they can affect you and your business.

Additional information can be obtained at: www.irs.gov/ep or call IRS: 877-829-5500 or call us for a free plan checkup

P: (908) 269-8878          Email: feberhart@investmentctr.com
F: (908) 269-8879          www.eberhartfinancial.com

**Notes:**

_____

_____

_____

# Plan Set-up Checklist

If you intend on starting a 401(k) or other defined contribution plan, you need a Plan Survey and checklist to help determine the proper type of plan and contribution and company matching percentages. The following questionnaire is designed to survey your employee's interest in establishing a company 401(k) Plan.

What is your level of interest in contributing on a pre-tax basis to the Plan if:

1. The company did not match
2. If the company matched your contribution:

| Company Match | Employee percentage contribution of payroll |
|---|---|
| 25% | _____% or dollar amount $_____ |
| 50% | _____% or dollar amount $_____ |
| 100% | _____% or dollar amount $_____ |

Would you like the plan to offer?
- Availability to take out loans
- Availability for hardship withdrawals
- Availability to transfer funds based on termination or retirement to an IRA or other qualified plan
- Vesting schedule for company match
- Investment Policy
- Type of investments or how many funds would you like to see
- Internet access to your portfolio's
- What are the costs to establish the plan, and what are the costs to maintain the plan?

**If you have an established Plan you should:**
(IRS required all plans to update the plan documents in 2010)
- Review Employee status
- Type of Plan
- Current Investment Manager
- Investment choices and performance
- Current Plan assets
- Any outstanding loans
- Recordkeeping and administrative expenses
- Timeliness of investment statements

- Look at educational levels provided, how were they provided and how often
- Provide educational and or investment review meetings
- Review your Plan documents for any IRS changes that may affect your Plan
- Review your Investment Policy

*In addition you need to:*
- Complete a current employee Census and any address changes send to the administrator or TPA
- Set up enrollment meetings with your Financial Advisor
- Non-discriminating Testing: Make sure your TPA (third party administrator) or whoever completes your testing for top-heavy salaried employees has completed the testing by March 15th to avoid excise on any refunds due.
- Form 5500 without any extensions the form must be filed by and signed by July 31st, by October 15th with an extension. Any Plans over 100 employees must have an independent auditors report for the 5500 filing
- Defined Benefit and Money Purchase Plans by September 15th
- Annual employer contributions to a defined contribution plan are due by March 15th, or September 15th with an extension
- Form 1099R for any distribution in the prior calendar year must be distributed by January 31st

# Annual Plan Limits

| Compensation | 2014 | 2013 | 2012 | 2011 |
|---|---|---|---|---|
| Limits on benefits and contributions | | | | |
| Defined contribution plans | $ 52,000 | 51,000 | 50,000 | 49,000 |
| Defined benefit plans | $210,000 | 205,000 | 200,000 | 195,000 |
| 401(k), 403(b), 457 plans | $ 17,500 | 17,500 | 17,000 | 16,500 |
| SIMPLE plan elective referrals | $ 12,000 | 12, 000 | 11,500 | 11,500 |
| IRA | $ 5,500 | 5,500 | 5,000 | 5,000 |
| | | | | |
| Catch-up Contributions | | | | |
| 401(k), 403(b), 457 plans | $ 5,500 | 5,500 | 5,500 | 5,500 |
| SIMPLE plans | $ 2,500 | 2,500 | 2,500 | 2,500 |
| IRA | $ 1,000 | 1,000 | 1,000 | 1,000 |
| Highly compensated | $115,000 | 115,000 | 115,000 | 110,000 |
| Key employee | | | | |
| Officer | $170,000 | 165,000 | 165,000 | 160,000 |
| 1% owner | $150,000 | 150,000 | 150,000 | 150,000 |
| Social Security wage base | $117,000 | 113,700 | 110,000 | 106,000 |

# [18]Types of Qualified Retirement Plans

A qualified plan must meet a certain set of requirements set forth in the Internal Revenue Code such as minimum coverage, minimum participation, vesting and funding requirements. In return, the IRS provides tax advantages to encourage businesses to establish retirement plans including:

- Employer contributions to the plan are tax deductible.
- Earnings on investments accumulate tax-deferred, allowing contributions and earnings to compound at a faster rate.
- Employees are not taxed on the contributions and earnings until they receive the funds.
- Employees may make pretax contributions to certain types of plans.
- Ongoing plan expenses are tax deductible.

**In addition, sponsoring a qualified retirement plan offers the following advantages**:

- Attract experienced employees in a very competitive job market: Retirement plans have become a key part of the total compensation package.
- Retain and motivate good employees: A retirement plan can help you maintain key employees and reduce turnover.
- Help employees save for their future since Social Security retirement benefits alone will be an inadequate source to support a reasonable lifestyle for most retirees.
- Plan assets are protected from creditors.

Employers can choose between two basic types of retirement plans: defined contribution and defined benefit. Both a defined benefit and defined contribution plan may be sponsored to maximize benefits. Our consultants can help you choose the right plan for your company. Listed below is a description of the types of plans that are available.

## Defined Contribution Plans

Under a defined contribution plan, the contribution that the company will make to the plan and how the contribution will be allocated among the eligible employees is defined. Individual account balances are maintained for each employee. The employee's account grows through employer contributions, investment earnings and, in some cases, forfeitures (amounts from the non-vested accounts of terminated participants). Some plans may also permit employees to make contributions on a before-and/or after-tax basis.

---

[18] Source: Preferred Pension Planning Corporation, Bridgewater, NJ

Frank J. Eberhart, CEP®, RFC®

Since the contributions, investment results and forfeiture allocations vary year by year, the future retirement benefit cannot be predicted. The employee's retirement, death or disability benefit is based upon the amount in his or her account at the time the distribution is payable.

Employer account balances may be subject to a vesting schedule. Non-vested account balances forfeited by former employees can be used to reduce employer contributions or be reallocated to active participants.

The maximum annual amount that may be credited to an employee's account (taking into consideration all defined contribution plans sponsored by the employer) is limited to the lesser of 100% of compensation or $51,000 in 2013 and $52,000 in 2014.

Tax deduction limits must also be taken into consideration. Employer contributions cannot exceed 25% of the total compensation of all eligible employees. For example, a company with only one employee earning $100,000 in 2012 would have a maximum deductible employer contribution of $25,000 (25% of $100,000). However, the employee could also make a $17,500 401(k) contribution to the plan. As a result the total amount credited to his account for the year would be $42,500 (42% of his compensation), and the contributions would meet the 2014 maximum annual limit since total contributions are less than $52,000.

## Profit Sharing Plans

The profit sharing plan is generally the most flexible qualified plan that is available. Company contributions to a profit sharing plan are usually made on a discretionary basis. Each year the employer decides the amount, if any, to be contributed to the plan. For tax deduction purposes, the company contribution cannot exceed 25% of the total compensation of all eligible employees. The maximum eligible compensation that can be considered for any single employee is $255,000 in 2013 and $260,000 in 2014. The contribution is usually allocated to employees in proportion to compensation and may be allocated using a formula that is integrated with Social Security, resulting in larger contributions for higher paid employees.

**Age-Weighted Profit Sharing Plans:** Profit sharing plans may also use an age-weighted allocation formula that takes into account each employee's age and compensation. This formula results in a significantly larger allocation of the contribution to eligible employees who are closer to retirement age. Age-weighted profit sharing plans combine the flexibility of a profit sharing plan with the ability of a pension plan to skew benefits in favor of older employees.

# 401(k) Plans

More and more employees perceive 401(k) plans as a valuable benefit which has made them one of the most popular retirement plans today. Employees can benefit from a 401(k) plan even if the employer makes no contribution. Employees voluntarily elect to make pre-tax contributions through payroll deductions up to an annual maximum limit $17,500 in 2013 and $17,500 in 2014. The plan may also permit employees age 50 and older to make additional "catch-up contributions" up to an annual maximum limit of $5,500 in 2013 and 2014.

The employer will often match some portion of the amount deferred by the employee to encourage greater employee participation, i.e., 25% match on the first 4% deferred by the employee. Since a 401(k) plan is a type of profit sharing plan, profit sharing contributions may be made in addition to or instead of matching contributions. Many employers offer employees the opportunity to take hardship withdrawals or borrow from the plan.

Employee and employer matching contributions are subject to special nondiscrimination tests which limit how much the group of employees referred to as "Highly Compensated Employees" can defer based on the amounts deferred by the "Non-Highly Compensated Employees." In general, employees who fall into the following two categories are considered to be Highly Compensated Employees:

- An employee who owns more than 5% of the employer at any time during the current plan year or preceding plan year (stock attribution rules apply which treat an individual as owning stock owned by his spouse, children, grandchildren or parents); or
- An employee who received compensation in excess of the indexed limit in the preceding plan year (indexed limit is $115,000 for 2013 and 2014). The employer may elect that this group be limited to the top 20% of employees based on compensation.

**401(k) Safe Harbor Plans:** The plan may be designed to satisfy "401(k) Safe Harbor" requirements which can eliminate nondiscrimination testing. The Safe Harbor requirements include certain minimum employer contributions and 100% vesting of employer contributions that are used to satisfy the Safe Harbor requirements. The benefit of eliminating the testing is that Highly Compensated Employees can defer up to the annual limit ($17,500 in 2013 and 2014) without concern for what the Non-Highly Compensated Employees defer.

## New Comparability Plans

New comparability plans, sometimes referred to as "cross-tested plans," are usually profit sharing plans that are tested for nondiscrimination as though they were defined benefit plans. By doing so, certain employees may receive much higher allocations than would be permitted by standard nondiscrimination testing. New comparability plans are generally utilized by small businesses who want to maximize contributions to owners and higher paid employees while minimizing those for all other eligible employees.

Employees are separated into two or more identifiable groups such as owners and non-owners. Each group may receive a different contribution percentage. For example, a higher contribution may be given to the owner group than the non-owner group, as long as the plan satisfies the non-discrimination requirements.

## Defined Benefit Plans

Instead of accumulating contributions and earnings in an individual account like defined contribution plans (profit sharing, 401(k)), a defined benefit plan promises the employee a specific monthly benefit payable at the retirement age specified in the plan. Defined benefit plans are usually funded entirely by the employer. The employer is responsible for contributing enough funds to the plan to pay the promised benefits regardless of profits and earnings. Employers who want to shelter more than the annual defined contribution limit of $51,000 in 2013 and $52,000 2014 may want to consider a defined benefit plan since contributions can be substantially higher resulting in fast accumulation of retirement funds.

The plan has a specific formula for determining a fixed monthly retirement benefit. Benefits are usually based on the employee's compensation and years of service which rewards long term employees. Benefits may be integrated with Social Security which reduces the plan's benefit payments based upon the employee's Social Security benefits. The maximum benefit allowable is 100% of compensation (based on highest consecutive three-year average to an indexed maximum annual benefit $205,000 in 2013 and $210,000 in 2014. Defined benefit plans may permit employees to elect to receive the benefit in a form other than monthly benefits, such as a lump sum payment. An actuary determines yearly employer contributions based on each employee's projected retirement benefit and assumptions about investment performance, years until retirement, employee turnover and life expectancy at retirement. Employer contributions to fund the promised benefits are mandatory. Investment gains and losses decrease or increase the employer contributions. Non-vested accrued benefits forfeited by terminating employees are used to reduce employer contributions.

## Cash Balance Plans

A cash balance plan is a type of defined benefit plan that resembles a defined contribution plan. For this reason, these plans are referred to as hybrid plans. A traditional defined benefit plan promises a fixed monthly benefit at retirement usually based upon a formula that takes into account the employee's compensation and years of service. A cash balance plan looks like a defined contribution plan because the employee's benefit is expressed as a hypothetical account balance instead of a monthly benefit.

Each employee's "account" receives an annual contribution credit, which is usually a percentage of compensation, and an interest credit based on a guaranteed rate or some recognized index like the 30 year Treasury rate. This interest credit rate must be specified in the plan document. At retirement, the employee's benefit is equal to the hypothetical account balance which represents the sum of all contribution and interest credits. Although the plan is required to offer the employee the option of using the account balance to purchase an annuity benefit, employees generally will take the cash balance and roll it over into an individual retirement account (unlike many traditional defined benefit plans which do not offer lump sum payments at retirement).

As in a traditional defined benefit plan, the employer in a cash balance plan bears the investment risks and rewards. An actuary determines the contribution to be made to the plan, which is the sum of the contribution credits for all employees plus the amortization of the difference between the guaranteed interest credits and the actual investment earnings (or losses).

Employees appreciate this design because they can see their "accounts" grow but are still protected against fluctuations in the market. In addition, a cash balance plan is more portable than a traditional defined benefit plan since most plans permit employees to take their cash balance and roll it into an individual retirement account when they terminate employment or retire.

## 401(k) plans

Is an employer sponsored tax-deferred savings plan for eligible employees. Separate accounts are maintained for employees, and the employer may offer a match for employee contributions. A 401(k) is a type of profit sharing plan; profit sharing contributions may be made in addition to or instead of matching contributions to the 401(k) plan. The employer may also allow loan or hardship withdrawal provisions.

*Plan Summary Highlights:*
- Employee, employer can contribute
- Employer may permit employee loans
- Employee withdrawals are permitted after 59 ½, or termination, death, disability or hardship if plan documents permit, any distribution is taxable
- 401(k) must be established before employee contributions begin
- Employee salary deferral contributions withheld and invested within 14 days of each established pay period
- Employer contributions must be made by tax filing date, including extensions
- Employer may exclude employees who work less than 1000 per year, under age 21, and have worked less than one year

- 100% of employee's money is vested immediately
- Employer contributions can be on a graduated vesting schedule
- Customize a plan design
- Employer is subject to IRS 5500 filings (plans that have never reached or exceeded an aggregate of $100,000 do not need to file a 5500), ADP, ACP, and top-heavy discrimination tests
- Costs run from $500 to $2500 for startups or take over plans, larger plans generally the startup may be waived, some fund companies offer a waiver to sign up, plus your administration fees for the TPA

**Profit Sharing Plans** are one of the most flexible plans for employers. A company can contribute to the plan on a totally discretionary basis. Every year the employer decides on how much, if any, will be contributed to the plan. In order to qualify for a tax deduction, the contribution amount cannot exceed 25% of the total compensation of all employees. The contribution is usually allocated to employees in proportion to compensation, and you may set up various types:

*Age Weighted* **formula** takes each employee's age and compensation. This will favor older employees who will receive a higher amount of the profit sharing contribution.

*Social Security Integration* generally results in higher amounts of the contribution to higher paid employees.

*New Age Comparability* or cross-tested plans are tested for nondiscrimination as though the profit sharing plan were a defined benefit plan (pension). The plan is utilized primarily by small business that wants to maximize the contribution of owners and highly compensated employees and minimize all other employee contributions. Comparisons of age weighted, social security integration, and new age comparability

**So how do you prepare for an audit? Best practices.**
1. Maintain a stand-alone ERISA policy, a one page notice that cross references your other policies and shows that you are thoughtful about ERISA and what your enhanced standard of care is for your plan clients.
2. Track all client accounts that are subject to ERISA.
3. Formalize your procedure for 408(b)(2) notices and updates.
4. Maintain model client documents that reflect current law. Review disclosures, RFP materials and make sure you have updated 404(a)(5) and 408(b)(2) notices.
5. Make sure all client service agreements are signed.
6. Develop a model response to plan clients for routine 5500 information requests. Make sure that what you disclose in your Form 5500 matches your 408(b)(2) disclosures.
7. For fiduciary services, ensure compensation is level. Are advisors or service personnel acting as functional advisors even if they don't hold themselves out as a fiduciary? Any fees for

services, variable compensation, revenue sharing and shareholder service payments, all of that would have to be offset or leveled against direct compensation. They want to make sure you don't have the potential to increase your compensation by the advice you give to your clients.

8. Referrals are fully disclosed and don't violate prohibited transaction rules.
9. Confirm that your affiliated and third party subcontractors are fully disclosed and do not violate prohibited transaction rules.
10. Provide ongoing education and training for your employees.
11. Include ERISA items in any internal audits.
12. Benchmarking. Look at the fees others are charging and make sure yours are reasonable.

There are four main reasons the DOL will single your firm out for an audit: **The DOL audit process can take six months to two years**

1. A participant complained to the Office of Participant Education, which is a DOL office similar to the SEC Office of Investor Education or Advocacy, about possible ERISA violations.
2. The IRS or SEC referred a case to the DOL.
3. The DOL used its National Enforcement Project, which looks at different providers and gathers information about the industry, to pick up low-hanging fruit in terms of audits.
4. Form 5500 filings. The new Schedule C requires plan sponsors to report compensation information that they received from providers. The DOL will look at plan sponsors to see if they are filing them correctly. If not, it is a way for the DOL to target providers.
5. 408(b)(2) requires that most service providers to retirement plans have to provide written disclosure of their services, fiduciary status and total compensation to the plan sponsors on an annual basis. The deadline for this disclosure to the plan sponsor is July 1, 2012. They have to include a description of the services provided and a description of the fee arrangement. The information can be delivered electronically and while there is no specific format required, the information provider must be in a format that is "sufficient to meet the guidelines." Service providers are continuing to work out the details of what that means. Plan sponsors are required to terminate any service provider who fails to information relating to future services. So 408(b)(2) covers the service provider to plan reporting obligation.
6. 404(a)(5) covers the plan to participant reporting requirement. That information includes general information about the structure and operation of the plan, as well as investment options, Plan sponsors must also provide an explanation of fees and expenses that are charge or deducted from participant accounts, including loans and other transactional fees. This statement is due the later of 60 days after the July 1, 2012 disclosure to the plan sponsor, or 60 days after the first day of the plan year beginning on or after November 1, 2011. While the final rules have a sample chart to use for disclosures, no specific format is required.

# Divorce and Business: Don't let the QDRO be Worse than the Marriage

Very few employers have any desire to get caught in the middle of the divorce proceedings of their employees; however, when company retirement benefits become part of the negotiations, unsuspecting employers can be pulled into the fray. One of the foundational rules for qualified retirement plans is that participants' benefits cannot be pledged as collateral or assigned to another party. Conditioning the plan's tax-favored status on this prohibition helps to protect participant benefits; however, there are a small number of exceptions to this rule. One such exception is that benefits can be included in marital property and assigned to a former spouse as part of domestic relations proceedings. This is accomplished via a Qualified Domestic Relations Order or QDRO.

## What Is a QDRO?

As the name suggests, a QDRO is a court order issued pursuant to state domestic relations laws (Domestic Relations Order or DRO) that is used to assign company provided benefits to an alternate payee, typically as part of divorce or marital separation proceedings. Although the rules governing QDROs are relatively straightforward, many divorce attorneys tasked with drafting them are unfamiliar with the nuances of qualified retirement plans. That can make an otherwise simple situation very complicated very quickly…and when dealing with the emotionally charged setting of a divorce, complication can lead to unpleasantness.

## Requirements

There are several key elements that must be included in a domestic relations order for it to be considered a QDRO.

## Identification of the Parties

The order must identify the plan, participant and the alternate payee, i.e., the party receiving benefits. This requirement is usually, but not always, easily satisfied. For example, an order that identifies the plan as the ABC Company's retirement plan may be sufficient if ABC Company has only sponsored a single retirement plan. However, if ABC has both a 401(k) plan and a cash balance plan, the order would be too vague without specifically naming the plan to which it referred.

Data privacy concerns have led many to discontinue including social security numbers as a means of identifying the participant and alternate payee, so there must be sufficient information included to ensure proper identification of all parties. This may be an easy task in most cases, but further detail may be needed if a participant's name is John Smith.

## Description of Benefits

The order must clearly articulate the amount of benefits to be paid or a formula for determining the benefits. For example, an order may require a participant to pay a former spouse $50,000. Alternatively, it may describe the benefit as 50% of the vested account balance as of a specified date. These two may be combined to ensure a minimum or maximum level of benefits, e.g., 50% of the vested account balance as of January 1, 2011, subject to a minimum amount of $50,000.

Then, there is the question of investment performance. If there is a lag between the determination date (January 1, 2011 in the above example) and the date the benefits are actually paid, the order should specify if the alternate payee is to share in any investment gains or losses during the interim.

## Purpose and Direction of Payment

A QDRO must provide child support, alimony or other marital property rights. Although the alternate payee is typically a spouse, former spouse, child or other dependent, benefits can be payable to another entity for the benefit of one of these parties. For example, the order may direct payment to a state department of family services to provide benefits for a participant's child.

## Prohibitions

Just as some items are required, other provisions will disqualify an order.

## Inconsistency with Plan Provisions

An order is not permitted to provide a type or a form of benefit or a benefit option the plan does not otherwise provide. For example, if a plan does not allow distribution in the form of an annuity, a DRO related to that plan cannot be qualified if it requires an annuity.

## Amount of Benefits

An order cannot provide benefits greater than the benefits available to the participant without the QDRO. For example, if a participant's account balance is $45,000, a DRO assigning benefits equal to $50,000 cannot be qualified. That is why many orders describe the amount payable as a percentage of the participant's benefits rather than as a flat dollar amount, especially in light of the economic volatility experienced over the last several years.

## Conflict with Previous QDRO

In the event a previous QDRO has assigned benefits to an alternate payee, a subsequent DRO cannot assign those same benefits to a different alternate payee. During 2010, the Department of Labor published new regulations clarifying this issue. The regulations specify that receipt of a DRO after an event such as a death or divorce or after receipt of another QDRO does not necessarily mean there is a conflict. Rather, the substance of the order(s) must be considered.

As long as payments under the first QDRO have not already commenced, a subsequent order modifying the amount is not, per se, a conflict. Similarly, if a participant who is already subject to one QDRO becomes subject to another, there is no conflict as long as the subsequent order does not attempt to assign the same benefits addressed in the first order.

## Processing

All plans are required to have procedures that describe how DROs will be processed and reviewed to determine their qualified status. Among other things, the procedure should specify the timing within which the review will take place and outline the flow of communication among the parties.

On receipt of an order, the plan sponsor should take immediate steps to freeze loans and distributions of the participant's benefits during the review period. The freeze should generally remain in effect until the earlier of:

- 18 months from the date the benefit was frozen
- The date distribution is made to the alternate payee
- The date the plan sponsor receives a court order releasing the participant's benefit from the freeze; or
- At the end of the 30-day appeal period that begins upon the alternate payee's notification the DRO has been denied if no appeal is filed.

## Don't Make Assumptions

While the rules described in this article are not necessarily complicated, the facts and circumstances of each situation bring unique details to be considered. As a result, each proposed QDRO should be reviewed carefully. Whether it is identification of the plan from which benefits will be paid or the calculation of the benefit itself or anything in between, any confusion should be clarified with the attorneys representing the parties.

It may be tempting to make assumptions in the interest of expedited processing; however, if those assumptions are incorrect and lead to improper payment of benefits, the plan sponsor may be held liable to make the parties whole. Although divorcing spouses are typically on opposite sides of the negotiation, they can unite very quickly against an employer who has incorrectly processed a QDRO.

## Death and Taxes

**Taxes:** As the saying goes, death and taxes are both unavoidable, and the same is true with QDROs.

When an ex-spouse receives distribution of plan benefits pursuant to a QDRO, he or she is responsible to pay the associated income tax. While this may seem obvious, both parties do not always understand that fact. Sometimes, however, the parties do understand and try to renegotiate the tax liability.

There was a Tax Court case in 1996 that dealt with this very issue. The QDRO in that case was written to shift the tax liability from the alternate payee (the ex-spouse) to the participant, but the Court held that the terms of a QDRO cannot override federal tax law and required the ex-spouse to pay the associated taxes. This does not mean that the parties cannot negotiate the principal amount of the QDRO payment to "gross-up" the alternate payee for the anticipated tax liability.

Distributions made pursuant to QDROs are generally taxed in the same manner as any other "typical" plan distribution (other than hardship distributions or required minimum distributions). The alternate payee has the option to receive payment in any form permitted by the plan, e.g., lump sum, installment, etc. He or she also has the option to take the payment as a cash-out or rollover into an IRA or another qualified plan. One key difference is that alternate payees who elect a cash-out distribution are not subject to the 10% early withdrawal penalty if the distribution is taken directly from the plan.

### Death

The potential for QDRO-related confusion does not always stop when payment has been made. It is not uncommon for a participant to assume that a QDRO officially concludes any right that his or her former spouse may have to retirement benefits. However, an ex-spouse may be listed as the participant's beneficiary. The federal courts see a number of cases each year involving "unintended" payment of death benefits. The typical scenario goes something like this…

A participant and second spouse go through a divorce, and the second spouse receives half of the participant's retirement benefits via QDRO. Fast-forward a few years to the participant's death. The participant has a will leaving all remaining assets to his or her children from the first marriage. However, the most recent plan beneficiary designation on file lists the second spouse as the primary beneficiary, because the participant forgot to file a new designation following the second divorce.

Since a beneficiary designation is considered a plan document, the sponsor follows the form on file and pays all remaining retirement benefits to the now-former second spouse. The children from the first marriage file suit, naming the second spouse and the plan sponsor.

While the facts of each case are unique, the plan sponsor in this fact pattern is generally correct in paying benefits to the person named on the most recent beneficiary designation form. The participant's will may determine how assets outside the plan are paid but it has no bearing on the payment of plan benefits. As a result, it is recommended as part of the QDRO procedure that plan sponsors remind participants to update their beneficiary designations.

## Summary

Divorces can be messy, and financial negotiations can make an already heated situation reach a boiling point. Understanding the rules of engagement and clearly documenting procedures can keep the plan sponsor's role to one of "just business" and minimize the liability associated with being pulled into the middle of an emotionally charged situation.

The information contained in this newsletter is intended to provide general information on matters of interest in the area of qualified retirement plans and is distributed with the understanding that the publisher and distributor are not rendering legal, tax or other professional advice. You should not act or rely on any information in this newsletter without first seeking the advice of a qualified tax advisor such as an attorney or accountant.

# Business Requirements Planning for SBA/Bank Lending

The following information is to assist anyone wishing to become self-employed. Regardless whether or not you apply for an SBA loan, Commercial bank Loan, local bank Loan-they will want this information. Secondly, you need to understand all that is involved for yourself. Use the above budget for business

As of _____, 2_____ **Personal/Business Financial Statement**

Name: _____

Business name: _____

Residence Address: _____

City _____ State_____ Zip Code _____

Business Phone: _____

Home Phone: _____

E-mail: _____

## Assets

| | | | Liabilities | |
|---|---|---|---|---|
| Cash | $ _____ | | Accounts payable | $ _____ |
| Savings accounts | $ _____ | | Notes payable (all) | $ _____ |
| IRA | $ _____ | | Installment Account | $ _____ |
| Life Insurance (cash value) | $ _____ | | Loan on life Insurance | $ _____ |
| Stocks/Bonds | $ _____ | | Margin amount (loan) | $ _____ |
| Real Estate (appraised) value | $ _____ | | Mortgage(s) | $ _____ |

*-List other real estate and mortgages on separate sheet (vacation home etc.)*

| | | | | |
|---|---|---|---|---|
| Auto | $ _____ | | Auto loan(S) | $ _____ |
| Personal property (art, jewelry) | $ _____ | | Loans against | $ _____ |
| Other assets | $ _____ | | Other liabilities | $ _____ |

**Income:** $ _____

## List of Required Documentation to Be Submitted with SBA Loan Application

The following information is required for an initial evaluation of an SBA Loan Application:

1. SBA Application from bank
2. Brief History of the Business. Discuss company history; description of business; product; market and customer base. Also, discuss the benefit the proposed loan will have on the business (form enclosed).
3. Debt Schedule for Business (form enclosed).
4. Resume (form enclosed).
5. Two (2) year Projection of Income and Expenses (form enclosed).
6. Format for New Business (form enclosed).
7. Personal Financial Statement for each principal (form enclosed)
8. Government Monitoring Information (form enclosed)
9. Personal Federal Tax Returns for each principal for the last three (3) years.
10. Financial Statement for the business for the past three (3) years, if applicable.
11. Federal Tax Returns for the business for the past three (3) years, if applicable.
12. Current Financial Statement for the business for a period ending within ninety (90) days of application.
13. Information in Items 10, 11 & 12 for any affiliate business.
14. If a Franchise operation, please provide a copy of the Franchise Agreement and FTC Disclosure Statement or Offering Circular with current financial information and literature for the Franchiser.

Please note that the SBA requires all of the above forms to be "signed" and "dated" by the appropriate individuals. After photocopying financial statements and tax returns, please sign again and affix current date.

## How to Apply for an SBA Loan Step-by-Step Procedure for a New Business:

1. Describe in detail the type of business to be established.
2. Prepare a resume describing experience and management capabilities.
3. Prepare an estimate of how much money you or others have to invest in the business and how much money you need to borrow. (Format for New Business).
4. Prepare a current personal financial statement.
5. Submit personal federal tax returns for the last three years.
6. Prepare a detailed projection of earnings for the first year the business will operate.
7. List collateral to be offered as security for the loan, indicating your estimate of the present market value of each item.

## For an Established Business:

1. Furnish amount of loan requested and the exact purpose for which it will be used.
2. Provide a brief description of the business and the benefits to be received from the loan.
3. Prepare a resume describing experience and management capabilities.
4. Submit business financial statements and federal business tax returns for the past three years, if applicable.
5. Furnish current interim business financial statement, if available.
6. Furnish a detailed projection of earnings for the next full year.
7. Furnish a current personal financial statement for all owners, stockholders and partners owning 20% or more of the business.
8. Submit personal federal tax returns for the last three years for the above parties.
9. List collateral to be offered as security for the loan, indicating your estimate of the present market value of each item.

## Purchase of a Business:

1. Describe in detail the type of business to be purchased and the reason for the sale.
2. Prepare a resume describing experience and management capabilities.
3. Prepare an estimate of how much money you or others have to invest in the business and how much money you need to borrow. (Format for New Business).
4. Prepare a current personal financial statement.
5. Submit personal federal tax returns for the last three years.
6. Prepare a detailed projection of earnings for the first year the business will operate.
7. List collateral to be offered as security for the loan, indicating your estimate of the present market value of each item.
8. Obtain the following information from the present owner:
   A. Current Balance Sheet and Profit & Loss Statement of business to be purchased.
   B. Last three years business income federal tax returns on the business being sold signed and dated by the seller.
   C. Proposed Bill of Sale including the amount, terms of sale, and an allocation of the purchase price.

Small business may look at factoring loans from credit card processors as a good alternative for funds, generally no personal guarantees, no application fees, 90% approvals and money within 72 hours. www.nabebankcardprocessing.com www.ebankcardprocessing.com

# Key Man Insurance for Business Owners

With many small businesses the key man or key employee in the business is the business owner. In these cases, key man life insurance can be purchased on the life of the business owner to protect the company in the event that he/she unexpectedly passes away. With key man insurance, the business owns the insurance policy and pays the premiums and is also the beneficiary. If the business owner dies, the business receives the policy proceeds and can use the funds to hire a capable replacement, pay off debts or simply use the funds to buy time until the businesses assets can be liquidated and the business can be closed. In any event, key man life insurance on the business owner can provide much needed stability if there is a sudden and unforeseen death.

## Life Insurance as Loan Collateral

Loans are crucial to the expansion and growth of small businesses. Whether your business is acquiring funds from a local bank, the SBA or a private lender, many of these institutions will require life insurance on the business owner(s) as security for the loan. In most cases, inexpensive term life insurance policies that offer guaranteed level rates for the duration of the loan can be purchased to satisfy this requirement. When buying life insurance to secure a loan, the company pays the premiums, owns the policy and is the named beneficiary.

As soon as the key man policy is effective, a collateral assignment agreement can be signed by the business owner and the bank. The collateral assignment is a lien against the policy proceeds. In the event of the business owner's death, the bank would have first rights to the policy proceeds in the amount of any outstanding loan balance due. The business would then receive any remaining proceeds. Every bank or lending institution as well as every insurance company has their own standard collateral assignment form.

## Buy-Sell Agreement Funding and Life Insurance

A buy-sell agreement is a legally binding contract which states that at an owner or partner's death, disability, retirement or otherwise separation from the company, the individual's interest in the company must be sold back to the business or to the remaining owners at agreed upon terms. These agreements are crucial for small and closely held companies, as in many cases, the death or disability of a business owner creates a significant financial burden on the business as well as the remaining partners. To limit this potential risk, most buy-sell agreements are funded with life insurance and or disability insurance policies. Depending on the type of buy-sell agreement, the business itself or the individual partner(s) acquires a policy on each owner/partner so that at death or disability the funds needed to "buy out" the individual's ownership interest are readily available.

# Employee Benefits

## Traditional, HSA, FSA, Self-Funded

For up to date information on ACA: https://feberhart.mybenefitadvisor.com

Health insurance is crucial for retaining and attracting employees as part of an employment package. The costs of traditional health insurance have been rising sharply over the last few years and now with all the new mandates for ACA (Affordable Care Act) it is becoming more difficult to maintain insurance policies for employees. In addition, effective 2014 all husband wife policies are no longer accepted, small business will be required to obtain commercial or corporate insurance (corporate welfare) to have at least 3 full time employees on payroll and able to produce a WR30 (employment salary verification). One Solution which is becoming increasingly popular (and misunderstood) is health savings accounts (HSA) which are high deductible out of pocket plans. It offers tax incentives to both the employer and the employee.

## ERISA Plan

The Employee Retirement Income Security Act (ERISA) of 1974 establishes minimum standards for retirement, health, and other welfare benefit plans, including life insurance, disability insurance, and apprenticeship plans. ERISA's extensive rules address the federal income tax effects of transactions associated with employee benefit plans, with mandates that qualified plans must follow to ensure that plan fiduciaries do not misuse plan assets. ERISA has been amended repeatedly since being signed into law. Also called the Pension Reform Act, ERISA protects the retirement assets of Americans. It is administered by the Employee Benefits Security Administration (EBSA), a division of the U.S. Department of Labor (DOL), along with the Department of Treasury and the Pension Benefit Guaranty Corporation.

## Who must abide by ERISA?

The protective laws under ERISA apply to employer-sponsored health insurance coverage and other benefit plans offered to employees by private employers (only). Corporations, partnerships, sole proprietorships, and non-profit organizations are covered, but governmental employers and churches are not, and are exempt from the application of ERISA. Up to now (under ACA-affordable health care Act) ERISA does not require employers to offer plans; instead it sets the rules for the plans and benefits which employers choose to offer. ERISA laws apply to privately purchased, individual Insurance policies or benefits *only if* (a) the employer allows those individual policies to be pre-taxed under a 125 plan, or (b) the employer endorses the policies as "voluntary policies" marketed and sold at the workplace.

## What ERISA Regulates:

ERISA refers to the full body of laws regulating employee benefit plans, which are found mainly in the Internal Revenue Code and ERISA itself. And must be managed in compliance with the various provisions mandated under ERISA, which include the following:

- Conduct: ERISA rules regulate the conduct for managed care (i.e., HMOs) and other fiduciaries (the person financially responsible for the plan's administration).

- Reporting and Accountability: ERISA requires detailed accountability and reporting to the federal government.

- Disclosures: Certain disclosures must be provided to plan participants (i.e. a written Plan Summary that clearly lists the benefits being offered, the rules for getting those benefits, the plan's limitations, and other guidelines for obtaining benefits such as obtaining referrals in advance for surgery or doctor visits).

- Procedural Safeguards: A written policy must be established to address how claims should be filed, and must detail a written appeal process for claims that are denied. ERISA also requires that claims appeals be conducted in a fair and timely manner.

- Financial and Best-Interest Protection: ERISA acts as a safeguard to assure that plan funds are protected and delivered in the best interest of plan members. ERISA also prohibits discriminatory practice when granting plan benefits to qualified individuals.

- ERISA has been amended to include two additional areas that specifically address health insurance coverage: the Consolidated Omnibus Budget Reconciliation Act of 1985 (COBRA) and the Health Insurance Portability and Accountability Act of 1996 (HIPAA).

*Failure to comply with ERISA's requirements can be quite costly, with possible DOL enforcement actions and penalty assessments and/or employee lawsuits resulting.*

## Are any businesses exempt from ERISA?

There are important statutory exemptions and regulatory safe harbors carving out plans that might otherwise fall within the ERISA plan definition.

Governmental and church plans are exempt from ERISA's mandates. Also exempt are programs maintained *solely* to comply with state-law requirements for workers› compensation, unemployment compensation, or disability insurance, as are plans maintained outside the United States for non-resident aliens.

- **Payroll Exemptions** certain payments are exempt if made as part of the employer's normal payroll practice. This includes payment of (1) wages, overtime pay, shift premiums, and holiday or weekend premiums; (2) sick-pay or income replacement benefits; and (3) vacation, holiday, jury duty, and similar pay. The key to this payroll-practice exemption: the amounts must be paid out of the employer's general assets and must be paid to currently employed individuals. Pre-funding (e.g., through Voluntary Employees' Beneficiary Association, or VEBA), use of insurance (e.g., insured short-term disability), or making payments (e.g., disability payments) to former employees can take an arrangement outside the exemption.

- **Voluntary Plans Exemption** The regulations also exempt certain "voluntary employee-pay-all" arrangements. Under such an arrangement, the employer allows an insurance company to sell voluntary policies to interested employees who pay the full cost of the coverage. The exemption permits employees to pay their premiums through payroll deductions and permits the employer to forward the deductions to the insurer. However, the employer may not contribute or endorse coverage and the insurer may not pay the employer for being allowed into the workplace.

## What is the most basic ERISA rule?

ERISA does not require an employer to provide employee benefits. Likewise, as a general rule, it does not require that plans provide a minimum level of benefits. Employers-sponsors are generally free to design their own benefits plans. Once an employer decides to provide benefits that are subject to ERISA, the plan's operation is regulated by ERISA, and the benefits must be detailed through a written ERISA approved plan document (called a Summary Plan Description-SPD).

Of course insurer documents should comply with all applicable legal requirements; insurers must provide adequate disclosures and notices, and must follow federal and state compliant claims procedures and applicable HIPAA regulations. Further, insurers assume responsibility only in regards to problems with insufficiency or inconsistency, or compliance failure with state regulations, not ERISA regulations. Most policies, certificates, summaries and other documentation produced and distributed by an insurer generally specify that the employer is the plan sponsor, plan administrator, agent for service of process, and the named fiduciary. In sum, it is the employer who is held accountable for any plan failures or compliance issues.

## The Employer is Responsible for Issuing Summary Plan Descriptions (SPDs) and Summary Materials Modifications (SMM)

Given that the employer-sponsor typically is the plan administrator, it follows that the employer (not the insurer) generally is responsible for furnishing Summary Plan Descriptions (SPDs), and that the employer will be held liable if adequate SPDs are lacking. SPD's must be furnished to each participant and to each beneficiary receiving benefits under the plan. DOL has authority to exempt any welfare benefit plan from all or part of the reporting and disclosure requirements. Under DOL regulations, the plan administrator of a *welfare* benefit plan is required to furnish SPDs (and SMMs) to participants *covered under the plan* only, and not to beneficiaries.

### Definitions of participant and beneficiary

By statutory definition, the term "participant" means an employee or former employee of any employer who is or may become eligible for benefits under an ERISA plan or whose beneficiaries are or may be eligible for benefits. Because the definition is not limited to current employees, it can include COBRA qualified beneficiaries, covered retirees, and other former employees who may remain eligible under a plan. The term participant does not specifically include a beneficiary, which is defined separately in ERISA to mean "a person designated by a participant, or by the terms of an [ERISA] plan, who is or may become entitled to a benefit there under." While beneficiaries typically include covered spouses and children, other individuals can become beneficiaries under the terms of a plan (e.g., a healthcare provider that receives an assignment of benefits under a patient's health plan). An alternate recipient under a qualified medical child support order (QMCSO) is treated as a plan participant for ERISA disclosure purposes. The SPD and SMMs must, therefore, be provided to these children. Generally, the SPD should be furnished to the custodial parent or guardian of a minor child. Under case law, SPDs and SMMs should be provided to a representative or guardian when the plan is on notice that the participant or other person entitled to an SPD is incapacitated.

### DOL only upon request

ERISA no longer requires the plan administrator to file a welfare plan's SPD or SMM with the DOL. However, these documents must be available for inspection upon request by the DOL and/ or plan participants.

**When there is a conflict between SPD/SMM and plan documents or insurance contracts** there are no initial penalties for failure to prepare or distribute a required SPD, unlike the case with Form 5500 reporting failures. Instead, repercussions from failing to have an adequate SPD arise when participants and beneficiaries sue to enforce plan rights. An inadequate SPD (for example, one that conflicts with the plan document it seeks to summarize) will normally be enforced by the courts in lieu of the underlying plan document, if doing so will favor the participant or beneficiary involved. In sum, without an adequate SPD in place employers can end up being liable for benefits they never intended to provide.

## ACA four-page summary of benefits and coverage required by Healthcare Reform

The healthcare reform law expands ERISA's disclosure requirements by mandating that a four-page "summary of benefits and coverage" be provided to applicants and enrollees before enrollment or re- enrollment. The summary (which we will refer to as the "four-page summary of benefits and coverage" or "four-page summary"), must accurately describe the "benefits and coverage under the applicable plan or coverage." The four-page summary requirement applies in addition to ERISA's SPD and SMM requirements. Although effective for plan years beginning on or after September 23, 2010, the four- page summary requirement contains a special distribution deadline of 24 months after the enactment of PPACA (March 23, 2010).

- The four-page summary requirement applies to health plans "grandfathered" in by health-care reform—that is, it is also a requirement of preexisting group health plans and health coverage.

- The healthcare reform law requires the Secretary of Health & Human Services to issue guidance (referred to as "standards") addressing the four-page summary requirement, and to do so by March 23, 2011 (i.e., 12 months after the enactment date). The standards are to be developed in consultation with the National Association of Insurance Commissioners (NAIC), a working group composed of (a) representatives of health insurance-related con-sumer advocacy organizations; (b) health insurers; (c) healthcare professionals; (d) patient advocates (including those representing individuals with limited English proficiency); and (e) other qualified individuals. Once developed, the standards are to be periodically reviewed and updated.

- The four-page summary requirement applies to group health plans and insurers (as defined by applicable provisions of the PHSA, ERISA, or IRS Code) but not to certain "excepted benefits." Grandfathered group health plans must comply with this mandate as well.

- The four-page summaries must be provided by plan administrators (for self-insured health plans) and insurers (for insured health plans). Note that a different rule applies in the case of SPDs and SMMs, for which ERISA plan insurers are never directly liable.

- Self-insured plans must prepare and provide the four-page summaries themselves or make arrangements with a third-party administrator to provide the notice on the plan's behalf. Finally, if the third-party administrator fails to provide the four-page summaries, the plan will be out of compliance and subject to penalties, as required under the healthcare reform law, despite its arrangement with the third-party administrator.

## ERISA /IRS reporting requirements
## (5500 are required for both 401K Plans and Welfare Benefits)

The primary reporting obligation ERISA imposes on welfare benefit plans is IRS Form 5500 annual report. The requirements:

1. ERISA also imposes an annual Schedule M-1 reporting obligation on multiple employer welfare arrangements (MEWAs) that provide health benefits. (Full title for Schedule M-1: *Reconciliation of Income (Loss) per Books with Income per Return.*)
2. In addition, if an ERISA welfare benefit plan uses a Voluntary Employees' Beneficiary Association (VEBA), the VEBA will be subject to a requirement under the IRS Code to file IRS Form 990, an annual information return. (Full title for Form 990: *Return of Organization Exempt from Income Tax.*)
3. Unless an exemption applies, ERISA requires the plan administrator of each separate ERISA plan to file an "annual report" with the DOL containing specified plan information. IRS Form 5500 is used for this purpose. ERISA authorizes the DOL to issue regulations exempting welfare plans from all or part of the Form 5500 reporting requirements, and the DOL has issued numerous exemptions for health and welfare plans. Unless an ERISA welfare plan qualifies for one of the enumerated Form 5500 exemptions, it must file Form 5500.
4. Small unfunded, insured, and combination unfunded/insured welfare plans" are, as noted above, completely exempt from the Form 5500 requirement. To qualify for this exemption, a plan must cover "fewer than 100 participants at the beginning of the plan year."
5. Under ERISA, penalties can be imposed by the DOL for any refusal or failure to file a required IRS Form 5500. Penalties may be assessed for late or un-filed Form 5500s as well as for incomplete or otherwise deficient Form 5500s.
6. ERISA §502 provides civil penalties for failure or refusal to file a required IRS Form 5500; for this purpose, a Form 5500 that has been rejected by the DOL for failure to provide material information will be treated as not having been filed. The penalties for noncompliance can be heavy: under ERISA §502, the DOL may assess a civil penalty against a plan administrator of up to $1,100 per day starting from the date of the administrator's failure or refusal to file the Form 5500.

7. The DOL takes the position that the penalties are cumulative so that the maximum per day penalty may be assessed for each Form 5500 that is not filed as required.

8. The DOL also apparently takes the position that it is not subject to a statute of limitations with respect to Form 5500. As such, it can assess penalties in connection with Form 5500 failures reaching as far back as the 1988 plan year (the first plan year following the ERISA amendment giving the DOL authority to assess Form 5500 penalties). Failure to correct a missed or incomplete Form 5500 may therefore leave the liability open and the potential penalty amount compounding.

9. The DOL maintains two programs under which penalties of less than the full statutory amount ($1,100 per day) may be assessed for compliance failures identified by the DOL: one concerns Form 5500s that are filed after their due dates and one concerns Form 5500s that are not filed at all.

10. Under the Late-Filer Enforcement Program, plan administrators may be assessed $50 per day for each day a Form 5500 is filed after its required due date (determined without regard to any extensions of time for filing). Under the Non-Filer Enforcement Program, "to reflect the egregious nature of the [non-filing] violation," a penalty may be assessed at a rate of $300 per day up to a maximum of $30,000 per year for each plan year filing.

## Section 125 Cafeteria Plan

A Cafeteria Plan (includes Premium Only Plans and Flexible Spending Accounts) is an employee benefits program designed to take advantage of Section 125 of the Internal Revenue Code. A Cafeteria Plan allows employees to pay certain qualified expenses (such as health insurance premiums) on a pre-tax basis, thereby reducing their total taxable income and increasing their spendable/take-home income. Funds set aside in Flexible Spending Accounts (FSAs) are not subject to federal, state, or Social Security taxes. On average, employees save from $.25 to $.49 for EVERY dollar they contribute to the FSA.

## Premium Only Plan (POP)

Employers may deduct the employee's portion of the company-sponsored insurance premium directly from said employee's paycheck before taxes are deducted.

## Flexible Spending Account (FSA)

In an FSA, employees may set aside on a pre-tax basis a pre-established amount of money per plan year. The employee can use the funds in the FSA to pay for eligible medical, dependent care, or transportation expenses

## Benefits to the Employer

Employers may add an FSA Plan as a key element in their overall benefit package. Because an FSA Plan offers a tax-advantage, employers experience tax savings from reduced FICA, FUTA, SUTA, and Workers' Compensation taxes on participating employees. These tax savings reduce or eliminate altogether the various costs associated with offering the plan. Meanwhile, employee satisfaction is heightened because participating employees experience a "raise" at no additional cost to the employer. Increased participation equals greater tax savings to the employer. Thus, to promote participation in the plan, employers may wish to contribute to each employee's FSA account.

## Benefits to the Employee

An employee who participates in the FSA must place a certain dollar amount into the FSA each year. This "election" amount is automatically deducted from the employee's check (for that amount divided by the number of payroll periods). For example, an employee is paid 24 times a year, and elects to put $480 in the FSA. Thus, $20 is deducted pre-tax from each paycheck and is held in an account (by the plan administrator) to be reimbursed upon request.

## Plan Year and Grace Period

The plan year is one full year (365 days) and generally begins on the first of a month. Many employers design their flexible spending plan to run on the same plan year as their insurance program. Short plan years are allowed in certain instances. The grace period is a timeframe up to 75 days after the end of the official plan year during which employees may use up any funds remaining at the end of the plan year. For example, if the plan year runs from July 1-June 30, the grace period for that plan may continue up to September 15. If an employee incurs an expense after June 30 but before September 15, they can utilize the remaining funds from the previous plan year and submit requests for reimbursement. In addition to the 75 day grace period, plan participants have an additional 90-day run-out period in which they can submit requests for reimbursement for expenses incurred during the dates of service within the plan year *and* grace period.

**Uniform Coverage** of Section 125 allows an employee to be reimbursed for qualified medical expenses that exceed their contributions to date. While this is a great benefit for the employee, it poses a potential risk to the employer. A case in point is when an employee terminates with a negative balance in their medical FSA. This risk should be offset because some other employees do not spend all of their FSA funds, so the risk is minimal. The rule states that for the medical expense account, a participant may claim the full amount of their annual election even if they have contributed only a portion of the total. For example, Sue Summers decides to contribute $480 for the year to her FSA account. To accomplish this, $20 is deducted pre-tax from each of her 24 payrolls for the year. Her plan starts in January. In March, Sue experiences a medical expense that costs $400. To date, she has contributed only $20 on six payrolls, meaning she has only $120 actual dollars in her FSA account. However, due to the uniform coverage rule she can claim and be reimbursed for the full $400 because of the assumption that her bi-weekly contributions will continue and she will eventually contribute the $480 total. This honor system is a huge advantage for participants, and allows them to experience medical expenses at any time of the year with no worry about having the funds available at the time the expense is incurred. Uniform coverage applies to the medical FSA only; it does not apply to a Dependent Care FSA. With a Dependent Care FSA account, a participant's reimbursement may not exceed the balance in the FSA account at the time the claim was made.

The Use-It-Or-Lose-It Rule states that any funds remaining in the participating employee's FSA account at the end of the plan year will be forfeited to the employer. Although the rule is clear, many users of an FSA largely misunderstand the result of the rule: loss of funds can be easily avoided. Let's look at an example: Joe Smith chooses to participate in the FSA and elects to fund $500 for the year. After the plan year and grace period are complete, Joe finds that he spent only $400 of the original $500 he put away. He fears he has lost $100, but due to the taxes he saved on the $500 he has not. Let's say Joe is in the 28% tax bracket. By putting $500 away in his FSA, he saved $140 in taxes (money that was not taken out of his paycheck and given to the IRS). In sum, even if Joe leaves $100 in his FSA account, he has still saved $40! This vital key issue must be explained completely too potential FSA participants. Employees who participate in an FSA should determine the amount to fund by looking at the expenses they will incur in a year; this amount is not an arbitrary number. In this example, let's say Mary Johnson is married with two school-age children. Mary has glasses and her husband Tom has allergies. When adding up how much to put away in her Medical FSA account Mary looks ahead for the year and determines that one child is going to need braces (add $5,000), that Mary is going to undergo LASIK surgery (add $3,000), and that Tom has a regular prescription for allergy medicine every month (add $120: $10 per month co-pay). Mary knows she'll have a few office-visit co-pays with the kids, too. Adding it all up, she determines she will put away $8,200 in her FSA. **These are expenses she knows will be incurred.** Once again, at an average 28% tax bracket Mary will save $2,296 by using her FSA! That is almost like getting her LASIK surgery for free! She has no doubt that she should take advantage of her FSA and save this money. Cafeteria Plans are qualified, non-discriminatory benefit plans, meaning a discrimination test must be met based on the elections of the participants combined with any contribution by the employer.

## Changes in Flexible Spending Accounts (FSA)

Nonprescription, over-the-counter drugs now require a doctor's prescription if they are to be eligible for reimbursement in an FSA (or in a Health Savings Account or Health Reimbursement

Arrangement). Further, the employer is responsible for compliance with these rules, which includes maintaining adequate records. Also beginning in 2011, the penalties have increased from 10 percent to 20 percent if funds from a Health Saving's Account are used for nonmedical expenses before age 65. Beginning in 2013, the maximum reimbursement amount will be limited to $2,500 for FSAs as part of a Section 125 plan. Currently, there is no Internal Revenue Service (IRS) limit on the amount that employees can defer on a pretax basis into a Flexible Spending Account. Meanwhile, companies on average impose a $5,000 limit, generally because the employer can become responsible for paying this amount, as shown in this example: employee opts to defer $5,000, in January employee undergoes surgery and uses the funds; the employer must provide the funds, even though said funds have not been taken from employee's paycheck yet. This scenario illustrates the problem which can arise when an employer reimburses an employee who then leaves the company before the funds can be collected through payroll contribution. By imposing a $2,500 cap, the plan generates the after-tax revenue while also presenting an opportunity for a cost savings to the employer.

**Nondiscrimination Testing** Section 125 of the Internal Revenue Code requires that Cafeteria Plans be offered on a nondiscriminatory basis. To ensure compliance, the Internal Revenue Code sets forth testing requirements that must be satisfied. These testing requirements are in place to make certain that Cafeteria Plan benefits are available to all eligible employees under the same terms, and that the Plan does not favor highly compensated employees, officers, and owners. Exceptions Sole proprietors, partners in a partnerships, and more-than-2% shareholders in an S-Corporation have special considerations concerning participation in a Cafeteria Plan.

[19]While sole proprietors cannot directly participate in the plan, they may legitimately employ their spouse and offer the spouse the benefits of the plan. In such instances, the employer must take care to ensure that the plan must be offered on a non-discriminatory basis. The employed spouse may be considered a highly-compensated employee and as such their contributions to the plan may be limited. A partnership operates much like a sole proprietorship. While the partners cannot directly participate, they may employ a spouse who in turn may receive benefits. The highly compensated issues apply as stated above. While all non-related employees may participate in the plan, depending upon the plan's parameters, non-discriminatory rules apply. In S-Corporations, eligible employees who are not shareholders and who are not defined as highly compensated generally may participate to the fullest extent. Eligible employees, who are defined as highly compensated, excluding shareholders, will be subject to the non-discriminatory rules. Special rules apply to a more-than-2% shareholder of the organization. These individuals may not participate in the plan; nor may their employee-spouse, children, parents, and grandparents. In determining the status of an individual that becomes or ceases to be a more-than-2% shareholder during the course of the S Corporation's taxable year, the individual is treated as a more-than-2% shareholder for the entire year.

---

[19] Check with your State as new requirements do not allow husband/wife to participate in corporate welfare benefit programs. You must have at least 3 employees full time on payroll.

**Section 105 Plan** of the Internal Revenue Service (IRS) regulations allows for reimbursement of medical expenses under an employer-sponsored health plan. There are various types of Section 105 plans including: Health Reimbursement Arrangements, Medical Expense Reimbursement Plans, Accident and Health Plans, and more. This allows for a self-employed individual to employ his/her spouse who is active in the business, and to offer that employed-spouse a medical benefits package. The benefits offered cover the employee, the employee's spouse, and the employee's dependents. This allows the self-employed individual to deduct 100% of his/her family's health costs from federal, state, and FICA/Medicare taxes. Standard tax law allows healthcare premiums to be deducted at 100% from federal and state taxes, leaving a substantial amount of potential tax savings on the table. Section 105 Plan allows a qualified business owner to deduct 100% of:

- Health insurance and dental insurance premiums for eligible employee(s) and family. This also includes qualified long-term care insurance.
- Uninsured (out-of-pocket) medical, dental, and vision care expenses for eligible employee(s) and family.
- Life, disability income, contact lens, hearing aid, Medicare Part A, Medicare Supplemental, optical/vision, and cancer insurance premiums for eligible employee(s).

## Qualified Filing Statuses

While the above rulings specifically address family employment in a sole proprietorship, corporations and partnerships may also take advantage of a Section 105 Plan. Additionally, employers seeking to offer non-related employees a medical benefits package may also implement such a plan. Here is how a Section 105 Plan works within the various filing statuses.

## Sole Proprietorships

Section 105 works well for sole proprietors who are able to legitimately employ a spouse who is active in the business. An employed spouse will be treated as any other employee, with the business owner offering medical benefits as part of the employee's compensation package.

## Partnerships

A partner in a partnership will operate similarly to a sole proprietorship. The spouse of the partner must be a bona fide employee, thus receiving the benefits of the plan. However, a partnership between a husband and a wife will not qualify for the plan.

## C-Corporations

Unlike the sole proprietorship or partnership, it is not necessary for spousal employment to occur within the corporation. The corporate entity may provide and deduct benefits for the owner-employee director. Although sometimes misunderstood, even if a business is incorporated, all the proper components must be in place in order for a Section 105 medical reimbursement plan to be in compliance with Internal Revenue Code, DOL, and ERISA.

## S-Corporations

While S-Corporations can qualify for a Section 105 Plan; special rules (defined by Revenue Ruling 91-26 and Announcement 92-16) apply to medical benefits paid to a 2% or greater shareholder. The special rules apply to shareholders only; employees not owning stock in the corporation may realize substantial savings by participating in a Section 105 Plan. Determination of actual savings depends on the facts and circumstances of each case.

## Limited Liability Company

Treatment of a Limited Liability Company (LLC) with respect to a Section 105 medical reimbursement plan depends upon how the entity files for purposes of its federal tax return. They may file as a partnership, a corporation, or a sole proprietorship. Once the filing status is determined, the appropriate rules for each filing status apply.

## Plan Year

Section 105 Plans generally run on a calendar (tax) year, January-December. Tax deductions are then taken during tax filing the following year.

## Carry Over

Revenue Ruling 2002-41 includes an option for a Section 105 Plan to manage and capitalize on future deductibility of unused portions of a medical expense account. If an employee does not use their maximum, they can carry it over to future years, insuring future deductions for "shock" years of healthcare expenses. The Carry Over applies to all employees on the plan. The maximum amount available under this benefit will accumulate over plan years and will be managed on an employee-by- employee basis. The business owner may choose to set a maximum Carry Over amount. Meanwhile, employees who utilize the Carry Over will have the amount available to them until the business ceases to exist, the plan terminates, there are zero Carry Over dollars remaining, or the employee becomes ineligible.

## Employee Compensation

**Under Section 105 Plan Check with [www.IRS.gov](www.IRS.gov) and** *Consult your tax professional for assistance with the requirements for filing all the appropriate forms.*

## Managing the Plan

The most important concept surrounding a Section 105 Plan is *legitimate employment* between spouses or any other named employee. This issue is closely scrutinized by the IRS, and it is absolutely vital that the relationship be in existence. Fabricated relationships are absolutely discouraged. Therefore, the following items must be in place to ensure the plan operates smoothly and the tax advantages are maximized:

- A written employment agreement.
- A log of hours worked by the employee.
- An established cash (salary) compensation payment amount and schedule.
- Name the insured (it is preferred that the insurance policy be in the employee's name).
- Maintain separate checking accounts (one for business use and the second for personal use).
- Pay for medical expenses (all medical expenses for the family should be paid by the employee from her/her personal account), and document all payments.

Notes:

_____

_____

_____

_____

_____

## SIMPLE Cafeteria Plan under ACA

Under the new Healthcare Reform package, effective for taxable years beginning after December 31, 2010, [20]small employers are now allowed to adopt new SIMPLE Cafeteria Plans. Under the new

---

[20] A small employer is defined as one with an average of 100 or fewer employees on business days during either of the two preceding years. If the employer was not in existence during the prior year, the determination is based on the average number of employees who are reasonably expected to be employed on business days during the current year.

law, SIMPLE Cafeteria Plans will be deemed to meet nondiscrimination requirements as long as the plan sponsor meets certain eligibility, participation, and minimum contribution requirements. This "safe harbor" would also cover the non-discrimination requirements applicable to certain benefits offered under a cafeteria plan, including group life insurance, coverage under a self-insured group health plan, and benefits under a dependent care assistance program.

A Cafeteria Plan (as provided for under Internal Revenue Code Section 125) is an employer sponsored plan under which employees have the option of selecting benefits or cash. Employees can choose which tax free benefits fit their needs, or may instead elect to receive taxable cash payments in lieu of unselected benefits. For example, under a Cafeteria Plan, employees may use salary reduction to pay their share of premiums for health insurance provided by their employer, with these payments made on a pre-tax basis. Thus, a Cafeteria Plan provides tax savings to employee and employer alike by subtracting premiums from gross salary before federal income and Social Security taxes are calculated. A Cafeteria Plan must be established in writing; it may not discriminate in favor of highly compensated participants and it may not favor key employees. In the past, these non-discrimination rules have discouraged small business owners from using Cafeteria Plans. Further, if the non-discrimination rules are violated the plan benefits provided to highly compensated or key employees must be taxed. Because of the potential for taxation of benefits provided by the plan, small employers—who may be more likely than larger employers to have a higher percentage of highly compensated employers— have tended not to provide Cafeteria Plans to their employees. In sum, besides easing the administrative burden once faced by small businesses that sponsored a Cafeteria Plan, the Healthcare Reform package also provides a safe harbor to the discrimination requirements applicable to highly compensated and key employees.

A SIMPLE Cafeteria Plan allows employees to use pretax funds to pay their portion of the health, vision, dental, and other employer-sponsored welfare premiums. The employer contribution must (a) equal a uniform percentage (not less than 2 percent) of the employee's compensation for the plan year, or (b) equal a 200% match of the employee contributions up to 6% of the employee's compensation for the plan year. The rate of match for highly compensated employees cannot exceed the rate of match for non-highly compensated employees. In order to meet nondiscrimination requirements, all non-excludable employees with at least 1,000 hours of service during the preceding plan year must be eligible to participate in a SIMPLE Cafeteria Plan. An employer may elect to exclude employees who have not attained age 21 before the end of the plan year, have less than one year of service as of any day during the plan year, are covered under a collective bargaining agreement, or are nonresident aliens. A plan may provide for a shorter period of service requirement for employees who are younger, if desired. Each eligible employee must be able to elect any benefit available under the plan under the same terms and conditions as those applied to all other participants.

## Who can benefit?

If an employer offers such a plan, the plan is deemed to pass discrimination testing. In discrimination testing, highly paid executives and other key employees' (as defined by regulations) benefits in the plan are compared to benefits provided to other employees who are contributing to the plan. If the plan does not pass certain threshold tests and therefore fails the test, benefits are refunded as necessary to the highly compensated employees and become taxable to them. For companies with a greater number of higher-level employees, such as a physicians' practice or a law firm, making the commitment to a SIMPLE Cafeteria Plan can allow key employees and executives to maximize their benefits by freeing them from discrimination testing. Another incentive to employers is the savings on payroll taxes. In addition, because the IRS may provide its own checklist in order to implement these plans, employers will save on plan document costs as well. Participation requires that employers make a minimum employer contribution, which means putting more dollars into the plan. With executives or key employees and discrimination testing issues, this slight drawback to the plan may be worth the investment.

**Employers should use a TPA to navigate complex SIMPLE Cafeteria Plans.** Utilizing these complex plans should consult professional guidance to ensure they are in compliance with the rules and understand the tax implications. SIMPLE Cafeteria Plan provides tax free benefits to employees. Healthcare Reform legislation did not change current law, in which sole proprietors, members of limited liability companies (LLCs), partners in a partnership, and more than two percent shareholders of S corporations are precluded from participating in a Cafeteria Plan. These restrictions will continue to be a major impediment to small business use of Cafeteria Plans.

Sources: http://feberhart.mybenefitadvisor.com www.eberhartfinancial.com

**Health Savings Accounts** (HSA) is an account established exclusively for paying qualified medical expenses incurred by the account participants. Individual and employer HSA plans are available. HSA plans allow employers and employees to make tax-free payroll contributions to their plan to pay for certain out-of-pocket medical expenses. By paying for these expenses on a pre-tax basis your employees increase their take-home pay without costing additional money. The employer saves payroll taxes for all participating employees. Any individual may establish an HSA only if they are first covered under a High Deductible Health Plan (HDHP). The employer must offer an HDHP in order to offer an HSA plan. Contributions to the HSA may be made on a pre-tax basis under a Section 125 Cafeteria Plan. Individual contributions are deducted pre-tax via payroll deduction. The employee, the employer, or both may make contributions to the HSA account. The non-discrimination rules applied to a Cafeteria Plan are the same for HSA contributions made under a Cafeteria Plan. This includes both employer and employee contributions.

Pre-tax funds are deducted via payroll deduction and deposited into a selected financial institution custodial account. When a qualified expense is incurred, the account generally has checks or debit cards, to pay for the expenses. Most custodial accounts (bank) offer investment options when the dollar amount reaches $2000 or more. Qualified medical expenses include costs for medical care as defined in Section 213(d) of the Internal Revenue Code. Health insurance premiums are not qualified medical expenses except for: qualified long-term care insurance, COBRA continuation healthcare coverage, and healthcare coverage while an individual is receiving unemployment compensation. Health insurance premiums or any portion the individual or employer pays are tax deductible and eliminate the 2% threshold rule on medical expenses. Exceptions are individuals enrolled in Medicare; they are ineligible because Medicare is considered other coverage that would disqualify the individual from being able to establish the HSA.

Medicare plans are MSA's www.cms.gov/medicare/health- plans/msa

## Health Reimbursement Arrangement (HRA)

A Health Reimbursement Arrangement (HRA) is a tax-advantaged benefit that allows both employees and employers to save on the cost of healthcare. HRA plans are employer-funded medical reimbursement plans. The employer sets aside a specific amount of pre-tax dollars for employees to pay for health care expenses on an annual basis. Based on the plan design, HRAs can generate significant savings in overall health benefits. The primary requirements for an HRA are that (1) the plan must be funded solely by the employer and cannot be funded by salary reduction, and (2) the plan may provide benefits for substantiated medical expenses only. HRAs may be designed in many fashions to suit the specific needs of employer and employees alike. It is one of the most flexible types of employee benefits plans, making it very attractive to most employers.

## Benefits to the Employer

HRAs are most commonly offered in conjunction with a High Deductible Health Plan. As a rule, moving to a High Deductible Health Plan will result in reduced premium costs, which creates real savings on healthcare costs for the employer. HRA contributions may then be funded using the savings gained from the lower premium costs. By funding an HRA, the employer effectively bridges the gap between the higher deductible and the expenditure amount at which the insurance coverage "kicks in" for their employees. Most importantly, all employer contributions to the plan are **100% tax deductible** to the employer, and tax-free to the employee. Employers may establish what expenses the HRA funds may be used for; from as comprehensive as all health-related eligible expenses to as limited as emergency room expenses only. Because they are very flexible, HRA plans enable employers to control costs of providing healthcare benefits while providing a valuable employee benefit. With an HRA, employee healthcare expenditures are visible and clear to employer and employee alike, thereby fostering a greater understanding of the costs of healthcare. In addition, employees who can monitor and control their healthcare costs become smarter healthcare consumers. Studies show that only 20-50% of employees actually use their healthcare coverage, meaning employers often pay health insurance premiums for employees who are not utilizing the coverage. An HRA allows employers to determine the best type of coverage for their employees based on the demographics of their employee group. HRA plans may also cover retired employees (and their spouses and tax dependents). Employers may wish to consider an HRA as an alternative to more expensive traditional retiree healthcare. Employee benefits, like an HRA, enable employers to recruit and retain quality employees. With an HRA in place, the employer is perceived in a positive light by current and prospective employees because a benefits package is being provided with the employee's interest in mind.

## Benefits to the Employee

Enrolling in an HRA provides two major advantages to employees: (1) a reduced health insurance premium resulting from the High Deductible Health Plan, and (2) availability of employer-sponsored funds to pay for medical expenses incurred prior to point at which the insurance deductible is met. Depending on the plan design, expenses that may be reimbursed from the HRA include the following: deductibles, co-payments, co-insurance, prescription medications, vision expenses, dental expenses, and other out-of-pocket health-related expenses. HRA funds are contributed to employees on a pre-tax basis; therefore, the funds are not taxable to the employee. As such, employees need not claim an income tax deduction for an expense that has been reimbursed under the HRA.

## Plan Designs

HRAs are very flexible, allowing the employer to design their plan to meet the unique needs of the company and the employees. Common plan designs include the following:

**Deductible, Co-pay, and Co-insurance:** All medical expenses that are applicable to the health plan's deductible, a co-pay amount, or a co-insurance amount qualify for reimbursement. Qualified expenses are those incurred by the employee or the employee's family. Explanation of Benefits (EOB) statement (provided by the employee's health insurance provider) showing evidence that the expense is applicable to the insurance deductible is typically required for substantiation of requests for reimbursement.

**Deductible:** All medical expenses that are applicable to the health plan's deductible qualify for reimbursement. This plan design does not include co-pays or co-insurance amounts. Qualified expenses are those incurred by the employee or the employee's family. An EOB statement is also typically required for substantiation of requests for reimbursement.

**All Uninsured Medical Expenses:** All out-of-pocket medical expenses (uninsured costs) are eligible. This includes deductibles, co-pays, coinsurance, dental, vision, prescription, and other out-of-pocket medical expenses. These expenses may be incurred by the employee or the employee's family. An EOB statement, copy of a receipt, or copy of a bill identifying the date of service, amount of service, and the name of the service provider are typically used to substantiate requests for reimbursement.

**Specific Expenses Only:** Plans may be designed to cover dental expenses only, orthodontia expenses only, vision expenses only, prescription medical expenses only, and/or other specified expenses. A copy of a receipt or copy of a bill identifying the date of service, amount of service, and the name of the service provider are typically used to substantiate requests for reimbursement.

**Plan Year (Period of Coverage)** Typically, employers choose to run the HRA concurrent with their health insurance plan year; this co-cycle is not mandatory and the HRA plan year may be independent of the health insurance plan year. Short plan years are generally available as well, depending on the options provided by the plan administrator.

**Carryover** with an HRA, unused fund amounts may be carried over from year to year. This differs from a Flexible Spending Account which maintains the "use-it-or-lose-it" rule. Employers have full discretion over how the carryover is managed. They may choose to allow the employee to keep all or only a portion of unused funds for use in later years, or may require forfeiture of all fund balances after the close of the plan year.

## Reimbursement

All requests for reimbursement under an HRA must be substantiated. The most common means of substantiation is the EOB statement provided by the employee's health insurance provider after a medical expense has been incurred. Since the HRA typically pays for out-of-pocket expenses up to the amount of the health insurance deductible, employees must reference the EOB statement to ascertain what has and has not been covered by insurance for a specific medical expense occurrence. They then request reimbursement for the portion of the expense that was not paid by their insurance plan. For other out-of-pocket expenses, a copy of a receipt or bill identifying the date of service, amount of service, and the name of the service provider is normally required to substantiate requests for reimbursement.

## Discrimination Testing and the Health Insurance Portability and Accountability Act (HIPAA)

Standard non-discrimination rules apply to an HRA. Plans must avoid discriminating toward any employee(s) regarding the parameters of the plan and how funds are allocated, and must ensure that all employees have similar access to a funded account. HIPAA privacy rules also apply.

**Coordination with a Flexible Spending Account** An employer may choose to offer a Flexible Spending Account (FSA) plan in conjunction with an HRA. An FSA is an *employee-funded* benefit that allows employees to set aside pre-tax funds to pay for medical expenses. FSA funds are contributed through salary-reduction, and the amount is determined by each participating employee. Combining an FSA with an HRA allows employees to bridge the gap between the employer sponsored HRA and the health insurance plan. In a situation where an incurred medical expense could be reimbursed from either the FSA or HRA, the employer or plan administrator will determine the "ordering rules" which determine which account the expense shall be reimbursed from first.

**COBRA** HRAs are subject to COBRA. Employees experiencing a qualified event must be given the opportunity for continued participation in the HRA offered by the employer. If an employee experiences a COBRA qualifying event and makes a COBRA election for the HRA, the employer determines the premium amount the employee must pay to continue participation. At the beginning of the plan year, the employer should establish a reasonable premium amount applicable to the HRA benefit being offered. This decision should consider the benefit offered for single vs. family. As the premium is determined at the beginning of the plan year, it cannot take into consideration an employee's account balance at the time of a qualifying event.

## Self-Funded Plans

Self-funding your organization's health care plan could reduce costs and improve overall service. More than half of U.S. employers are fully or partially self-funded. And now many insurers require only 5 employees to qualify. Self-funding may not be right for every organization. Employers considering a switch from fully-funded to self-funded health plans should carefully consider the pros and cons before switching from traditional to fully or partial self-funding.

## Definition of a self-funded plan

According to the Self-Insurance Institute of America, Inc., a self-funded group health plan is one in which the employer assumes the risk for providing health care benefits to its employees. Instead of paying a fixed premium to an insurance carrier, self-funded employers pay employee health care claims out of their own pockets as the claims are incurred. For multi-state employers, self-funding can help create national consistency by eliminating the need for state-by-state compliance.

## Benefits of self-funded plans

The disadvantages of self-funding are the assumption of greater risk. A year that brings large, unanticipated medical claims can be devastating to employers with poor cash flow. Another obstacle to self-funding is the need for strong administrative skills. While many self-insured organizations use third-party administrators or enter into "administrative services only" arrangements with an insurance company. The U.S. Department of Labor (DOL) has interpreted the failure of self-funded employers to implement an efficient administrative system as a breach of fiduciary duty. Evaluate stop-loss insurance options. Most self-funded employers purchase stop-loss insurance that provides protection against costly claims. Stop-loss coverage can be triggered by either a high dollar claim or by surpassing a predetermined aggregate claim amount, depending on the type. Under the first, an employer may buy a policy that shifts responsibility for a claim to the insurer once it exceeds a certain dollar amount, such as $10,000 or $20,000. Under the second, the insurer assumes responsibility once the total amount of claims for all employees reaches a specific threshold. Companies approaching self-funding with a long-term perspective are more likely to do well with self-funding. Because claims are cyclical, they need to make a three-to-five year commitment to see savings."

HHS issued final rules on "essential health benefits" required under the Patient Protection and Affordable Care Act ("PPACA"). The rules are important for the future of state and federal health insurance exchanges as they finalize rules with which insurance companies must comply in providing benefits to their employees. **However, these essential health benefit rules do not apply to self-funded medical plans.** In fact, many PPACA rules do not apply to self-funded plans. Because of the differences in the rules governing self-funded plans versus those governing fully insured plans, some employers who have not previously thought self-funding was a better approach to providing health care benefits are now revisiting the issue.

## Potential Self-Funding Savings

One of the primary reasons why employers are considering self-funding today is the cost savings that may result from self-funding. Self-funded plans escape the health insurance industry fee under PPACA, the proceeds of which are used to fund state and federal health insurance exchanges. The cost will run 2% to 2.5% of premiums in 2014. Self-funded plans also avoid the essential health benefits mandates of PPACA. These services include ambulatory patient services; emergency services; hospitalization; maternity and newborn care; mental health and substance use disorder services, including behavioral health treatment; prescription drugs; rehabilitative and habilitative services and devises; laboratory services; preventive and wellness services and chronic disease management; and pediatric services, including oral and vision care. One large insurance company estimated in 2012 that the services mandated for fully insured plans by PPACA will increase premiums from 7.5% to as much as 15%.

Self-funded plans also avoid state premium taxes, which cost participants and employers around 1.75% of premiums each year. A self-funded plan could have savings as much as 20% over a fully insured plan.

Other advantages to self-funding are:
- Self-insured plans are not tied to community rating for determining premiums as are insured arrangements.
- Self-funded plans will be more adept at allowing employers to determine what their true costs of coverage are. With this data, employers can more directly address high cost services.

- Medical loss ratio requirements do not limit self-funded plans' expenditures on administrative expenses as they will for insured plans.
- Self-funded plans are likely to be in a better position to manage future uncertainty because they escape greater regulation that the health insurance industry faces.
- Review of premium increases by the Secretary of HHS under the health care reform law does not apply to self-funded plans.
- Self-funded plans avoid the adverse selection insured plans are likely to encounter.

A self-funded plan creates opportunities for small and mid-size companies to enjoy all the benefits of a self-funded plan with less risk. Most of the benefits the employees receive are:

- Lower out of pocket limits
- Generally 100% coverage after deductible and any coinsurance are met
- The incentive is for controlling costs, besides the above mentioned savings, when the stop loss provision is established, let's say $20,000 and the benefits paid out during the year were only $12,000, the company receives the difference from the stop loss of (in this case $8000) of which they can take the money or encourage the employees to use their health care more wisely and the company can redistribute the money for all employees by lowering their premiums the following renewal period. By using an insurance carrier, they have the use of their TPA (administrative services) fees built into the plan.

## Self-funded Terminology guidelines you should understand:

- Administration: Sales and general expenses Fees for overall administration of the self-funded plan. I.e. Enrollment and eligibility maintenance, billing, ID cards, PPO fees, claim administration, anti-fraud services, document preparation, customer service and broker commission.

- Aggregate Stop Loss: Protects the employer from unusually high aggregate claims. Eligible claims for all covered persons that are greater than the annual aggregate attachment point during the contract period are paid by aggregate stop loss insurance. If the stop loss insurance contract terminate prior to the end of the contract period, the aggregate stop loss insurance coverage is no longer in effect and the employer is liable for all eligible claims.

- Annual Aggregate Attachment Point: The overall claim dollar liability limit of the employer during the contract period. All eligible claims in excess of this amount are paid by aggregate stop loss insurance.

- Claim Processing: The employers claim prefunding responsibility during the contract period up to the annual aggregate attachment point. If there is a claim prefund surplus at the end of the contract period a portion of the claim prefund may be available in the form of a refund or fund future plan administrative expenses.

- Minimum Annual Aggregate Attachment Point: The minimum dollar amount of aggregate eligible claims under the self-funded plan which the employer is responsible during the contract period.

- Run Out Period: The period of time immediately following the termination of the stop loss insurance contract in which the insurance company will continue to process eligible claims incurred during the contract period.

- Specific Stop Loss Insurance: protects the employer from unusually large claims of a particular person covered under the self-funded plan. Eligible claims for each covered person that are more than the specific deductible during the contract period are paid by specific stop loss insurance.

- Stop Loss Premium: the fee for specific and aggregate stop loss insurance coverage.

**Notes:**

_____

_____

_____

_____

_____

# Marketing Tips

## What separate's your business from everybody else?

- Service
- Ethics
- Reliability
- Value
- Integrity
- Contact
- Extraordinary Product Selection
- Services and products that fit your clients needs

Back to basics, how do you get in front of clients, once you are in front of them how are you going to sell them? I go back to my roots, seminars, workshops, making appointments for face to face selling.

So, my formula for success: **FABASS**

- F: Features
- A : Analysis
- B: Benefits
- A: Advantages
- S: Sold
- S: Keep it Simple

**Here are a few additional items that could make the difference:**

- Branding your name, company logo
- Professional web site, using SEO development for Google searches etc.
- Professional business cards, flyers, and literature
- Join various organizations, Chamber of Commerce, LinkedIn, Facebook, Twitter, Yelp, Manta, etc. One of the biggest followings is Twitter.
- Do trade shows
- Subscribe to e-magazines, magazines
- Do workshops and seminars
- Chamber of Commerce events and workshops may provide other avenues of gaining new clientele.
- Join school boards or other local organizations.
- Support local sports programs, charities, etc.

## Market Your Target
## You need to understand and define the type of market you want

Demographics play a large role in workshops and or seminars, individuals generally will only travel more than 10-15 minutes from home or work to attend. Secondly, if it has no interest nobody will attend.

So when you send out an invitation for a seminar, workshop, or webinar, have an agenda that will attract their attention.

With so many email market campaigns, (I get hundreds a day-and generally do not open them as an attachment), I go back to my roots, direct mail, seminars, and workshops. I do some email campaigns through places like LinkedIn or Facebook, Manta, and "opt in" email campaigns such as Vertical Response, Constant Contact, etc. where it is visible before you open any attachment.

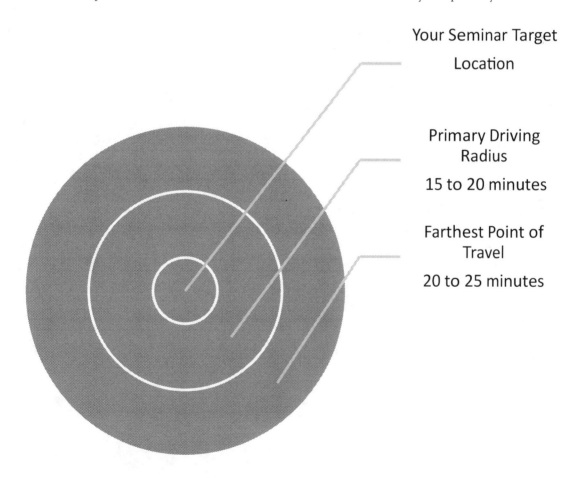

Your Seminar Target Location

Primary Driving Radius
15 to 20 minutes

Farthest Point of Travel
20 to 25 minutes

When conducting a workshop or seminar, keep it to one hour or less and for workshops focus on a specific topic (Don't wander). I use my workbook to do a workshop on retirement or estate planning. This lets me focus to my strongest topics; you need to refine your workshops and seminars to do the same. YOU need to be the main speaker, not any guest speakers you may bring-the audience needs to bond with you and your business.

As an example (I did a lot of seminars, and email blasts) a formula I used for mailers:

Sample 5" × 8" Mailer (Back)

Multi-Strategy Portfolio Development

Trust & Investment Management

Annuities & Life Insurance

Wealth Management

Portfolio Review

Estate Planning

Bonds

Eberhart Financial Services Group, Inc.

P: (908) 269-8878 F: (908) 269-8879

E-mail: feberhart@investmentctr.com

Web site: www.eberhartfinancial.com

Always include your phone number, e-mail, and Web site address in the return address.

Eberhart Financial

699 Washington Street, STE 302

Hackettstown, NJ 07840

(909) 269-8878

Web site: www.eberhartfinancial.com

E-mail: feberhart@investmentctr.com

Use printed label for client address

One 8.5 x 11= 2 post cards

# SEO (search engine optimization) and Your Business

## Just because you have a web site doesn't mean they can find it

First buy a **DOMAIN** name: http://www.melbourneit.com.au or http://www.godaddy.com

Second: If you accept credit cards, check payments, internet, recurring (automatic billing), plug n pay (client logs in and pays), wireless, phone swipe, or desk top: establish a merchant account: www.nabebankcardprocessing.com

- When individuals search the web and hit a link (your web site), they are there for around 1.5 seconds, if nothing catches their eye-they are gone-probably never to return. As an example when you visit my web: www.bookworm.tv the moving image catches your eye, and I change topics, structure quite often. I provide information that makes them come back, like the mortgage calculator, retirement calculator, etc.

- Second problem is load time, if it takes too long to load your web image-gone

- Third problem is broken links, a picture of your web page(s) it is actually what a web search engine sees, if it is blank-gone.

- Fourth problem is linking your site to other links-check out frame page vs. link page.

- Fifth is setting up your search criteria, like Google. Finding key words, phrases, and topics. If you are not on the first or second page when an individual Google's, then they usually do not go to the third. If you Google Frank Eberhart, I am probably the first 20 pages. So practice, go to Google and type in criteria that matches you, see what or where you land-front page? Be as specific as possible.

- Learn google+ and google analytics.

- It is not the number of hits; it is the number of unique visitors and search engines look for IAAT (In Anchor and Title) and KEI (Key Word Effectiveness Index) the higher both of these numbers the better.

- There are others for sure, Google is a great tool to find some

- It is not the number of hits; it is the number of unique visitors and search engines look for IAAT (In Anchor and Title) and KEI (Key Word Effectiveness Index) the higher both of these numbers the better.

- There are others for sure, Google is a great tool to find some

www.netmechanic.com is a search engine optimizer. $99 dollars a year you can subscribe to over 100 search engines all at once and they give you a report back on which search engines accepted (and ones you may have to go in and manually subscribe to). They offer additional services like broken link repair, Meta tabs (only 4 or 5 Meta tabs or it becomes spam) which are key words and phrases that attach to the top of your actual web site. A very valuable and inexpensive tool.

For web site ranking:
- www.alexa.com www.googleanalytics.com
- www.adwords.google.com
- www.searchmarketing.yahoo.com
- http://www.keyworddiscovery.com

www.blogger.com (Google), what can I say-its Google and they have really great services and applications to help promote you and business.

http://blogtalkradio.com

You need to understand and target your market, geographical boundaries, and your client

# Quick Reference List of Web Pages

| | |
|---|---|
| www.lifehappens.org | Life insurance calculator |
| www.irs.gov | Internal Revenue Service |
| www.irs.gov/govts | Federal/state/local Web pages |
| www.bankrate.com | Compare CDs, calculators, credit lines, and more |
| www.ssa.gov | Social security |
| www.medicare.gov | Medicare |
| www.adviserinfo.sec.gov | Investment adviser public disclosure |
| www.irahelp.com | Investments |
| www.morningstar.com | Mutual fund rating |
| www.personalfund.com | Mutual fund rating |
| www.investinginbonds.com | All about bonds |
| www.bondschool.com | Education on bonds |
| www.finra.com | National Association of Securities Dealers |
| www.andrewtobias.com | Mutual fund ratings |
| www.findlaw.com | National legal Web site |
| www.giftlaw.com | Gifting |
| www.treasurydirect.gov | Buying U.S. treasury bonds direct |
| www.publicdebt.treas.org | Debt and other services |
| www.bls.gov/cpi/home.htm | Bureau of Labor statistics (tracking the CPI |
| www.savingforcollege.com | College 529 Web page |
| www.cnnmoney.com | Financial Web page |
| www.sec.gov/cgi-bin/srch-edgar | Securities Exchange Commission (SEC); unaudited mutual fund, annuity, and company information Web page |
| www.ipx1031.com | 1031 exchange intermediary |
| www.amex.com | American Stock Exchange for Options |
| www.nyse.com | New York Stock Exchange |
| www.sec.org | Securities and Exchange Commission |
| www.nfa.futures.org | National Futures Association |
| www.cftc.gov | Commodities Futures Trading Commission |
| www.sec.gov/answers/annuity.htm | SEC Web page for annuities |
| www.horizoninvestments.com | Dynamic asset allocation money manager |
| www.ira.com | IRA Web page information |
| www.bigcharts.com | A stock tracking site |
| www.nicep.org | National Association of Certified Estate Planners |
| www.iarfc.org | National Association of Registered Financial Consultants |
| www.iuniverse.com | My other book publisher |
| www.archwaypublishing.com | Archway Publishing my book publisher |
| www.nareit.com | National Association of REITs |
| www.hud.gov/offices/hsg/sfh/hecm/rmtopten.cfm | Reverse Mortgage Web page |

| | |
|---|---|
| www.acli.org | American Council of Life Insurance |
| www.nlm.nih.gov/medlineplus/nursing homes.html | National Library of Medicine |
| www.medicare.gov/nhcompare/home.asp | Health and Human Resources |
| www.irs.gov/uac/Form-706 | Federal Gift Tax web |
| http://www.house.leg.state.mn.us/hrd/pubs/estatesurv.pdf | State estate, gift tax, inheritance tax |
| http://www.irs.gov/pub/irs-pdf/i1040tt.pdf | Federal Estate Tax |
| www.bookworm.tv | my author website |
| http://feberhart.mybenefitadvisor.com | my business web site |
| www.eberhartfinancial.com | my business web site |
| www.nabebankcardprocessing.com | my credit card business web site |
| www.ebankcardprocessing.com | my merchant cash advance web site |

# Glossary

## Financial Definitions

*AON:* All-or-none orders are limit orders in which you want to fill the entire order or none of it.

*Annual report:* A document that summarizes the operations and performance of a company for its fiscal year. By law, the report must contain the company's business and disclose its income, profits, losses, and net worth.

*Annuity:* A contract sold by an insurance company that guarantees the annuitant (owner), or his or her beneficiaries, a series of fixed or variable payments.

*Arbitrage:* Profiting from buying a security that costs less than normal and immediately selling it for profit.

*Asset allocation:* Placing several asset classes of investments to offset volatility.

*Basis point:* 100 basis points are equal to 1 percentage point.

*Bear market:* A period of declining stock values.

*Benchmark:* A standard, such as the S&P 500, for money managers or mutual funds to measure their success.

*Bonds:* Fixed income securities that are loans by the investors to companies and governments in return for a fixed amount of payments and agreed interest (coupon rate). The yield is the actual amount you get when held to maturity; if a bond is called early, the yield to call price is your real return.

*Book value:* The difference between what a company owns and what it owes.

*Bull market:* A period of rising stock market values.

*Capital gain:* Money earned on the sale of an asset (selling price minus cost). If less than one year has passed since the purchase, the gain is taxed as ordinary income; after one year, the gain is currently taxed at 15 percent.

*Capital loss:* The money lost from the sale of an asset or a security.

*Certificates of deposit (CDs):* These follow the federal fund rate and are insured through the Federal Deposit Insurance Corporation (FDIC). For more information, visit www.bankrate.com.

*CDSC charges:* Back-end load, typically with class B shares. The deferred sales charge can be as high as 6 percent over a declining scale of typically six years.

*Closed-end fund:* A fund that issues a limited number of shares that trade like a stock. Share prices rise and fall with demand and can sell for more or less than its NAV.

*Commission:* A fee charged by brokers (stock brokers, real estate brokers, and so on) for services rendered, such as buying and selling a stock or bond.

*Commodities:* Bulk goods-such as grains, foods, and metals-that are traded on a commodity exchange.

*Compounding:* The growth of interest on the principal plus previously earned interest.

*Distributions:* The payments a fund makes to investors from sales of securities held in the fund, interest, and dividends. It equals the fund's return (or loss) to shareholders. Typically, the fund companies reissue additional shares versus cash distributions.

*Expense ratio:* The charge you pay for your total investment, including management fees, operating expenses, trading costs, sales charges. Check out the average cost and history of funds at www.andrewtobias.com, www.personalfund.com, and www.morningstar.com.

*Fill or kill:* An instruction to cancel the order if it is not executed immediately.

*Front-end load:* An up-front sales charge (commission) to your mutual fund. Sales charges vary from 3.5 percent and up; this is in addition to manager fees, redemption fees, distribution fees, taxes, and any 12b-1 fees the fund may charge.

*Futures contract:* An agreement to purchase or sell a commodity or security at a predetermined price and date.

*Good-'til-canceled (GTC):* Orders that are in effect until executed.

*Index fund:* A fund that imitates the performance of a stock index, such as the S&P 500.

*Inflation:* An increase in the price of goods and services passed on to the consumer.

*Insider trading:* The buying or selling of stock by anyone who has nonpublic information (information not released to the public) that could affect the price of the security.

*Institutional investor:* An organization-such as a bank, mutual fund company, insurance company, pension fund, or money manager-that buys large volumes of securities.

*IPO:* Initial public offering of a company's stock.

*Insurance:* A contract with an insurance company in which the company agrees to pay a dollar amount for death or disability to an estate or individual in exchange for premiums (dollars).

*Interest rate:* The cost of borrowing money.

*Investment objective:* All funds must have an investment objective-income, growth, balanced, and so on. The objective must be stated in the prospectus.

*Margin:* Borrowing money against a security such as stocks, bonds, or mutual funds.

*Mortgage rates:* Generally tied to ten-year treasury bonds. Adjustable-rate mortgages, home equity lines, and credit lines follow the prime rate.

*Net asset value:* The closing price of each trading day by taking the total value, subtracting expenses, and dividing by the total number of shares outstanding.

*Open-end fund:* A fund that continually issues more shares.

*Par value:* The face value of a bond ($1,000) that can be redeemed or called at par.

*P/E ratio:* The price of a stock divided by the earnings per share.

*Pension:* A fund established by an employer to provide a set amount of income when an employee retires.

*Prospectus:* The official document describing a mutual fund. It must accompany any sales offering to a client prior to or within a reasonable time period before purchase of the shares.

*Proxy:* An authorized individual who votes on specific agendas of a company. Shareholders are issued proxies.

*Redemption fee:* A charge that may be applied to liquidation of shares held for a short period of time. B or C shares typically carry redemption fees.

*Short selling:* The process of an investor borrowing shares of stock from a broker and hoping the stock will drop in price. The investor buys shares of the same stock when it drops and replaces the borrowed shares for a profit.

*Stock split:* A company splits its stock (generally two for one) to attract more investors, and then hopes the value of the company appreciates. If the stock price was $100 per share and it split two for one, the new price would be $50 per share.

*Spread:* The difference between the bid and offer price of a security.

*Securities Investors Protection Corporation (SIPC):* The organization that insures brokerage assets (generally $100,000 in cash, $400,000 in securities). Most brokerage houses offer additional insurance protection in case of default.

*Triple witching day:* The third Friday in March, June, September, and December. This is when options, index options, and futures contracts expire at the same time.

*Zero coupon bond:* A bond that is sold at a deep discount and pays no interest. The holder collects the full face value of the bond at maturity.

## Estate Definitions

*A/B trust:* Also called a marital trust or bypass trust. A trust to place your unified credit exemption. The A trust is for a living spouse; the B trust is for a deceased spouse.

*Administrator:* Person the court names to administer the estate.

*Adjusted gross income (AGI):* Income less adjustments.

*Alternate beneficiary:* Person who receives assets if the primary beneficiary dies.

*Alternate valuation date:* Date that is not to exceed six months after the date of death. The value of the assets must be lower than, and result in, a reduction of the gross estate to qualify.

*Alternative minimum tax (AMT):* A tax calculation to ensure that individuals and trusts do not escape federal tax liabilities. You or your tax adviser needs to calculate regular income tax and AMT and pay the highest tax.

*Ancillary administration:* Probate of property or assets in another state (unless in trust).

*Annual exclusion:* The annual amount in each taxable year that you may gift to an individual. As of December 31, 2001, this was $13,000 per individual, $26,000 per married couple filing jointly.

*Asset allocation:* The proper investment mix for an investor, based on time frames, goals, needs, objectives, and risk tolerances.

*Assignment:* Transferring your interest in any asset to another party. Used commonly in trusts.

*Basis:* What you paid for an asset. Determines taxes for gains and losses.

*Beneficiaries:* The individuals or corporations that receive assets from the estate after probate or from trust.

*Bequest:* A specific gift by will of a designated class or kind of property.

*Certificate of trust:* Verification of the trust. It explains the powers of the trustee and identifies any successor trustees.

*Charitable gift:* Gifts of cash or property to a qualified charity in which the donor receives tax deductions, income, and estate and capital gains benefits.

*Class A beneficiary:* Examples are mother, husband, wife, father, son, and daughter.

*Class B beneficiary:* Examples are cousin, aunt, uncle, nephew.

*Codicil:* An amendment to a will.

*Conservator:* An individual (guardian) legally responsible for the care of another individual.

*Contest:* To dispute the terms of a will.

*Corporate trustee:* An institution that manages assets for a trust.

*Corpus:* The principal property of a trust.

*Creditor:* The individual or corporation that is owed money.

*Crummy power:* The power held by the beneficiary to withdraw a certain amount of money annually from the trust.

*Custodian:* The individual who manages assets for minors under the Uniform Gift to Minors Act (UGMA).

*Defined benefit plan:* A corporate-sponsored retirement plan.

*Defined contribution plan:* An employee-funded retirement plan, sometimes matched by the employer-e.g. 401(k), 403(b).

*Disclaimer provision:* The allowance of the beneficiary (generally the surviving spouse) to refuse acceptance of certain assets for federal tax purposes.

*Durable power of attorney (financial):* Allows full or partial authority of an individual to make decisions and transact business on your be-half in the case of incapacitation. The appointment can be by will pro-visions, trust instruments, or court appointment.

*Durable power of attorney (health care):* Allows full or partial authority of an individual to make decisions for health care in the event that you are unable to do so (you are incapacitated). The appointment can be by will provisions, trust instruments, or court appointment.

*Dynasty trust:* An irrevocable life insurance trust (ILIT) used by weal-thy individuals to create a nontaxable generation, skipping transfers for several generations.

*Equity:* The current net value of an asset.

*Employer stock option plan (ESOP):* A defined contribution plan in-vesting in the employer's stock.

*Estate:* The total value of all assets of an individual or individuals. Used to determine estate taxes and state death taxes as determined by an independent appraiser for IRS purposes.

*Estate taxes:* Federal taxation on the assets in an estate less the unified credits and debts. Federal estate taxes are net; state death taxes are from the gross estate.

*Executor:* The person or institution named to carry out the instruction set forth in the will or trust instrument.

*Fiduciary:* The person or institution that has the legal right to act for another person, generally in financial matters.

*Funding:* The process of transferring assets into your trust.

*Gain:* The difference between what you paid for an asset and what you sold it for (capital gain).

*Generation-skipping transfer (GST):* An exemption that allows you to transfer property or cash for two or more generations for inheritance purposes. This is currently at $1.1 million each (indexed for inflation).

*Generation-skipping transfer tax:* A transfer tax assessed on gifts in excess of $1.1 million to grandchildren and great-grandchildren. The tax is at 55 percent.

*Gift exclusion:* The annual amount allowed per individual to gift to another individual in each calendar year (currently $13,000 for individuals, $26,000 for married couples filing jointly). Commonly used to fund GST, legacy trusts, life insurance trusts or Crummy trusts.

*Gift tax:* currently 35 percent that the IRS imposes on any gift exceeding the annual gift exclusion (currently $13,000 per year per person to anybody). Penalties can range from 200–400 percent, plus the current percent gift tax.

*Grantor:* The person who establishes the trust. Also called the donor.

*Heir:* An individual entitled by law to receive part or all of an estate.

*Incapacity:* The state of an individual who is no longer capable of handling his or her own affairs for medical or financial reasons. This can be permanent or temporary. It generally requires court intervention and supervision to protect the individual from wrongdoing.

*Inheritance:* The assets received from the net proceeds from an estate.

*Inter vivos:* A trust established while you are alive.

*Irrevocable life insurance trust (ILIT):* A trust established to own life insurance policies and remove them from your taxable estate. It pro-vides tax-free and estate tax-free dollars to your beneficiaries.

*Irrevocable trust:* A trust that cannot be revoked or cancelled.

*Intestate:* Without a will.

*Joint tenants with rights of survivorship (JTWROS):* Property that transfers automatically to the surviving spouse. The assets are now taxable in the surviving spouse's estate.

*Living will:* A will that states whether or not you wish to be kept alive by artificial means if permanently injured or ill.

*Medicaid:* A federal program in which you trade assets for nursing home care.

*Medicare:* A federal health care program for individuals over sixty-five who are covered by social security.

*Pour-over will:* A will stating that any assets left outside your living trust will become part of your living trust.

*Power of attorney:* A legal document giving an individual or corporation power to transact business on your behalf.

*Probate:* The court process of validating your will, paying debts, and distributing assets according to the wishes of your will.

*Qualified terminal interest property trust (QTIP):* Assets transfer into the QTIP trust on the death of the donor and provide income for the surviving spouse. It assures that the remaining assets will transfer to the rightful heirs.

*Qualified personal residence trust (QPRT):* The QPRT trust holds the title to the donor's primary residence (or vacation home), and the do-nor retains the right to live there for a specified period of time. It re-moves the property from the estate.

*Revocable trust:* A trust that allows the donor to change, revoke, or cancel the trust any time.

*Special needs trust:* A trust established to take care of an individual who is not capable of doing so for himself or herself.

*Spendthrift trust:* A trust that protects assets from creditors and restricts or limits spending by the beneficiary.

*State death tax:* A death tax imposed on estates in addition to federal estate taxes.

*Step-up in basis:* An asset that has passed through probate or from a trust. The new value is considered the new basis moving forward for tax purposes for the heirs. Generally, it avoids capital gains and gift taxation after passing through probate or from a trust.

*Successor trustee:* The individual or institution that takes over as trustee should the first trustee die, resign, or become incapacitated.

*Testamentary trust:* An unfunded trust inside a will. It does not avoid probate and could trigger gift and capital gains taxes.

*Testate:* Having died with a will.

*Testator:* An individual who leaves a will in force at death.

*Trustee:* An individual or institution that manages and distributes as-sets for another or for oneself as in the case of a revocable living trust.

*Unified credit:* The exclusion from federal estate taxes currently 5.120 million reducing to 1 million in 2013

*Will:* A written legal document administered and distributed through the probate process, according to your instructions.